Big Data War

Big Data War

How to Survive Global Big Data Competition

Patrick H. Park

BEP BUSINESS EXPERT PRESS

First published in 2016 by
Business Expert Press, LLC
222 East 46th Street, New York, NY 10017
www.businessexpertpress.com

ISBN-13: 978-1-63157-560-0 (paperback)
ISBN-13: 978-1-63157-561-7 (e-book)

Business Expert Press Big Data and Business Analytics Collection

Collection ISSN: 2333-6749 (print)
Collection ISSN: 2333-6757 (electronic)

Cover and interior design by S4Carlisle Publishing Services
Private Ltd., Chennai, India

First edition: 2016

10 9 8 7 6 5 4 3 2 1

Printed in the United States of America.

Abstract

Written by Patrick H. Park, an author of *Brain Work* (Korea, 2014). The book mainly focuses on why data analytics fails in business. It provides an objective analysis and root causes of the phenomenon, instead of abstract criticism of utility of data analytics. The author, then, explains in detail on how companies can survive and win the global big data competition, based on actual cases of companies.

Having established the execution and performance-oriented big data methodology based on over 10 years of experience in the field as an authority in big data strategy, the author identifies core principles of data analytics using case analysis of failures and successes of actual companies. Moreover, he endeavors to share with readers the principles regarding how innovative global companies became successful through utilization of big data. This book is a quintessential big data analytics, in which the author's know-how from direct and indirect experiences is condensed.

How do we survive at this big data war in which Facebook in SNS, Amazon in e-commerce, and Google in search expand their platforms to other areas based on their respective distinct markets? The answer can be found in this book.

Keywords

Amazon, Apple, big data, business intelligence, consulting, customer analysis, customer profiling, CRM, data, deep learning, Facebook, Google, IT, machine learning, MBA, marketing, product profiling, problem solving, strategy, Tech, Venture

Contents

Prologue

"That's a nice hat!"

That's what the grown-ups said in *The Little Prince* written by Antoine de Saint-Exupéry, when they saw the drawing that the child who grew up to be the pilot drew of a boa constrictor that had swallowed an elephant. From the child's perspective, he had drawn a boa constrictor, but looking at it from their own perspective, grown-ups concluded that it was a drawing of a hat.

Would there ever be a grown-up who figures out that the drawing is of a boa constrictor that swallowed an elephant? Nonetheless, the child's drawing was that of a boa constrictor. Naturally, the child with his idea of a boa constrictor and the grown-up with his or her idea of a hat have a huge communication gap; consequently, there are limits to how close they can get to each other.

No matter how well the child explains about the boa constrictor that swallowed an elephant, grown-ups are likely to find it difficult to understand its meaning. Is it possible for a snake to swallow an elephant from a commonsensical perspective? What if the child does not even explain the drawing? No matter for how long a grown-up talks with the child and looks at the drawing, it seems that there is little possibility for the grown-up to understand the child's intention and share the child's joy of the drawing.

Data analytics is a similar story. Currently, with the growing amount of information and significant growth in the big data market, many companies brag about the huge amount of data they have and emphasize that it is the future asset of the company. Can the potential of the data then be realized? Wouldn't they be forgotten at some point without realizing their potential?

Although no one doubts the potential of big data, they are useless unless they are delivered as some kind of a value to humans. To find an answer to the question of how to provide value, we need to deliberate on what is in people's minds first.

Many companies try to do something big with "big" data, but what is valuable to humans is not that complicated, and contrary to common belief, this does not require all that much data. Although a grown-up called "data" appears to understand everything because of having a lot of knowledge, the grown-up may be completely oblivious to the possibility that the interest of the child called "human" is a boa constrictor.

According to a forecast by IDC, a market research company, the size of the 2018 global big data market would reach about $41.5 billion. However, behind this gigantic growth, a dark shadow exists. The results of a survey conducted by Gartner, an IT consulting company, showed that three-fourths of all big data projects failed.

Have you ever heard of a case of a company that became successful because of data analytics? Some media coverage would have you believe that this is true, with cases of novel data analytics, but cases of substantial success are extremely rare. This is because many companies still see big data technology from a grown-up's rather than a child's perspective.

The companies that attempt big data analytics, regardless of industry, first pile up a massive amount of data and plunge into the analysis project enthusiastically. They bring in huge data servers and analytic solutions, along with all available cutting-edge techniques. However, as the project progresses, their initial enthusiasm is nowhere in sight, and team members just want the project to be wrapped up reasonably well. As they approach the closing of the project, no one talks about project results. This is because there is no result. When finally asked about the results, they reluctantly give vague responses such as "there is a potential" or "gained new insight."

Countless companies have conducted data analytics such as business intelligence (BI) and customer relationship management (CRM) in the past, but a case that has generated clear results is nonexistent. What is the reason behind their failures? The biggest reason was because "goal setting" did not come first. Projects that explore goals from data always fail. Data are nothing more than a "tool"; therefore, I always stress the following when analyzing big data:

"Clarify the goal first. Then, let data be led by the goal. If the goal is led by data, it is bound to fail."

PART 1

Dump the Data

CHAPTER 1
Global Data War

The Era of the Ant Winning Over the Grasshopper

The story "The Ant and the Grasshopper" from *Aesop's Fables* is about an ant that spends the warm seasons gathering food for winter and a grasshopper that spends its time singing and lazing around; when winter comes, the hungry grasshopper begs the ant for food, and the ant criticizes the grasshopper's laziness.

Does the story of the ant and the grasshopper, where one gathers diligently in order to succeed, reflect the situation in today's modern business world? At least in the area of big data, the situation is actually the opposite! This is because in modern business, companies that spend freely rather than gather diligently win the race. This is an incomprehensible situation from the point of view of production-centered economic perspective plagued with a "growth obsession" that existed in the past. Yet it is true—the modern big data war is the war of "spending."

The current age is the era of material and information excess; anyone can access information easily and use it freely. It is no longer the age of material growth, of production based on large facilities and capital, as in the past. In modern industries, data is like an energy resource, and data analytic capacity is like an engine of the company. In the future, industries which do not utilize data will neither be competitive nor grow.

In contrast to the past, when hardware-oriented companies used to grow, nowadays only the service and IT industries based on software are growing. While world economy in the 20th century was driven by big brick-and-mortar corporations such as GM, US steel, and Exxon, in the 21st century, knowledge-based service companies such as Facebook, Amazon, and Google dominate the global market.

In the case of hardware industry, only the companies that step closer to the needs of consumers by combining software and hardware technologies are surviving. These companies are trying to get a competitive edge by using products such as wearables and smart cars in order to gather data and thus use customer customer-oriented data analytics. In the current era, not only data analytics for manufacturing but also data analytics for understanding people is essential. This is because all companies are moving toward personalization.

From Information Technology to Data Technology

What is the growth engine of companies in the current era? Most companies stress data analytics as the core competency for growth. More precisely, the key is to use a business model where there is a convergence of engineering and humanities, and where data analytics rather than algorithms are used for creating value.

In the current IT ecosystem, global enterprises have two major battles. The first is the "platform war," the battle to monopolize data by securing a customer base and by external growth, and the second is the "data analytics war," the battle to have a competitive edge so as to maintain a virtuous cycle and continue growth.

In the early 2000s, global IT companies established absolute power in their respective fields through traditional services such as social network services, e-commerce, and web-search. However, as services converged, and with hardware integrating into services as well, conflict in the service platforms those companies were based on was inevitable, and eventually, they will have to get together and face the war that will determine their survival.

In the platform war, the companies that secure customer base and data first have absolute leverage. Strictly speaking, the platform war is a traffic war. Let's think about it from the customers' point of view. Once the time spent on working or studying as well as sleep is excluded, the time left to spend on platform services is very limited. If a company secures this span of time and the platform on which services are provided, it can make profit from expanding and providing services such as advertisement, retail, media, and finance. Conversely, companies that lose customer contact point become powerless and are reduced to providing mere infrastructure support. As a result, in the current management environment, only platform companies that hold the "key" to customers can survive. Therefore, in the present era, traffic—the amount of customer activity—determines the value of a company.

If that be the case, what should companies do to secure a customer platform? First of all, companies must see customers at eye level. They must move away from supplier-centered management and study consumer-oriented services. Aggressive expansion of services does not guarantee success. No matter how good the weapons are, companies without skills are bound to lose. We can see in the case of Evernote, which expanded and started offering diverse services, losing customer-centered core competencies.

The ability to understand customers comes from data analytics. To become competitive using a platform and ultimately control the market, companies must create services by analyzing data. In the end, the final goal of companies is to provide customers with *personalized platform and service*. The core of software power is big *data analytics capabilities*.

Declaration of War among Global Enterprises

Facebook, a social network service (SNS) company, is a case in which the company started by securing a customer base using a network of acquaintances, and then, created a revenue model using data analytics. Starting a service based on a simple idea of networking within Harvard University, Facebook created a virtuous cycle of expanding customer base effortlessly by securing a large volume of traffic. Soon dominating the entire United States and expanding to the global market, Facebook has focused until recently on development of network algorithms that find close friends or gatherings.

Having solidified the platform and building barriers against competitors' entry, Facebook is now steadily expanding using data analytics. Moving beyond finding acquaintances, Facebook is providing various Internet services that can be used based on network data such as applications, news, games, advertisements, and shopping services that fit individual customers. It creates value by identifying customers' hidden needs and bringing in appropriate services from outside. For this, Facebook is concentrating its efforts on identifying customer needs, focusing on behavior characteristics of individual customers.

Amazon, an online retail company, in its early days of business, focused all its effort on simply attracting demand and supply. The company succeeded in attracting influential retailers by publicizing the company to ordinary consumers, and took over the online retail market by creating a virtual cycle of network concentration. Now, expanding its online retail services worldwide, and also moving into transportation and manufacturing industries, Amazon is strengthening its superior platform status in the market. To ensure traffic, it has also acquired entertainment businesses which could stimulate customer interest.

An important point here is that the core competency of Amazon also comes from data analytics. Amazon's ability to perform the role beyond a mere retail platform came from its aggregation and analysis of customer activity data. Amazon is utilizing the information obtained from analysis, such as customer purchase pattern analysis and association analysis, in a variety of ways including personalized recommendations, search algorithms, and grouping based on customer types. To increase traffic, it has also stepped into new areas such as fresh food and fashion based on analysis of services sensitive to customer inflow and corporate strategizing using data analytics. This can be considered a prime example of complementary role of platform expansion and data analytics.

Google, an Internet service company, initially established its customer base using a search technology called PageRank. It became the ultimate winner, more or less, of the search market, and secured major revenue sources (advertisement), and it is currently making efforts to expand the platform in various ways. Following the period of being primarily focused on Internet users' basic needs, Google has gradually expanded its customer base through operating system (OS), cloud computing, e-mail, office products, and content. To secure the traffic of customer contact points, Google also acquired YouTube, a media company.

Google is attempting to get into more intimate spaces of human life through platform expansion in combination with hardware. It is approaching consumers in different ways as it develops data analytics services linked to smart cars and IOT, and develops algorithms for problems such as machine learning and robotics. It appears to be a natural that Google clashed with other platform companies such as Amazon and Facebook.

These examples of global IT service companies in the 2010s, such as Facebook, Amazon, and Google, show that as these companies expanded their platforms to other areas from their distinct base markets of SNS, e-commerce, and web-search respectively, their service areas began to clash. They began competing in terms of platform expansion and data analytics, and tried to acquire key high-tech companies and recruit talent. That is literally a war! It should be noted that as hardware and process algorithms are standardized now, increasing competitiveness and service development based on data analytics has emerged as a significant factor more than ever.

The management environment of the large corporation of the past can be no longer viable. In large companies, it is difficult to yield results by implementing and utilizing data analytics because business and IT are separated. However, many companies have excellent infrastructure and manage large data through computerization. This has sufficient growth potential. We are just desperately in need of data scientists who can create masterpieces by orchestrating data and talents.

How to Survive the War

We must find the best way through examination of past failures in data analytics. My focus in this book is to determine precisely the "causes" of failures of data analytics. Instead of abstract criticism of utility of data analytics, this book focuses on objective analysis of the phenomenon and finding a root cause. This will be the first step toward success of data analytics.

Data Analytics without a Goal Fail

Based on my experience, a distance between business goals and big data exists in many companies. Why does the distance exist? In most companies, data analytics is considered as "exclusive work of the IT department." That is, data analytics is defined from a systemic perspective as a mere "auxiliary to the main functions" of companies, which is primarily based on statistical analysis.

On the other hand, innovative companies view data analytics and business in equal standing. To achieve business goals, they process data and link it directly to outcomes. The success of big data does not depend on the amount of data or specifications of hardware. Success is determined by whether data is viewed passively and used only for materials, or actively, utilizing it to solve problems.

Data analytics is not just an IT engineer's role—developing programs based on a superiors' orders for long hours in a computer lab. Data analytics is an activity that determines strategic direction by shaping the future core competencies, and is the agent for conducting corporate activities in an orderly fashion. The end stop of data analytics is human and business. Handling data to fit human value is the only way for the modern company to survive. This requires talent that combines humanities and engineering.

Find the Boa Constrictor in the Child's Mind

The insight to approach data from the "human-centered" viewpoint in order to provide practical assistance for "human" life determines the future of a company. Recognizing the boa constrictor in the picture requires getting in the child's head foremost. As such, services that are valuable to humans are not simple algorithms; we cannot rely solely on scientists and engineers. Only the data analytics that combines humanities for understanding of business and human, based on statistics and computer engineering, can create real value.

However, in reality, many high-tech companies have difficulty in recruiting the talents who have both competencies in humanities and engineering. This puts a challenge in creating a convergence business model for data analytics.

"Dump the Data, If You Want to Make Data Analytics a Success."

To a person holding a hammer, everything looks like nails. Those who hold data tend to solve all business problems with just data. If this continues, they become locked in a narrow way of thinking, and eventually fail. We need to drop the hammer, and look at the problem. At some point, we will find ourselves holding a hammer and ultimately will take control of data.

Success Built by Data, Will Be Destroyed by Data?

"You would have no idea how colossal the Tesco tragedy was."

That is how Mike Bird, a reporter from *Business Insider*, described the fall of Tesco. Accomplishing a remarkable growth by meeting customer needs and supplying products at best prices at the right place and time based on sophisticated data analytics, Tesco was a legend in the field of data analytics. However, recently announcing enormous drop in revenue, Tesco admitted a failure in data-based management. Tesco announced an annual pre-tax loss of £6.4 billion in 2015. This was one of the biggest losses recorded in the history of UK companies. Moody's, an international credit rating agency, downgraded Tesco's credit rating to Ba1, and its share price hit the lowest level since 2000.

Is Data Analytics Really a Mirage?

In the field of data analytics, and especially in the retail industry, few companies have been successful with data analytics. As it was revealed that data analytics, which had once excited many with symbolic cases such as "beer and diaper" (noticing that many husbands shopping for diapers buy beer along with diapers, the two products were displayed next to each other), does not generate outcomes despite its flashy outside, the argument that "data analytics is useless" became widespread. As a result, many marketing companies based on data analytics disappeared. In this context, Tesco's success felt like a rain after a drought to believers of data at the time.

Tesco, which has been on a winning streak based on successful data analytics in the early 2000s, collapsed in the end. Watching the failure of the company considered the exemplar of retail data analytics, many experts gave a sigh, saying, "As expected, data analytics won't do it." The personnel from the failed company also sometimes justified their failure by stating, "Data analytics is not meant to be sustainable."

Did Tesco's revenue drop because of data analytics? If so, how was Tesco's growth in the early 2000s possible? Most marketing strategies at the time of Tesco's growth were established based on customer data analytics. The value of data analytics clearly existed. Before jumping to a conclusion that the failure of Tesco was due to data analytics, let us take a look at causes of failure.

Data Alchemy of Tesco

Tesco, the largest retailer in the UK which grew to become a global retailer, began as a small supermarket. The size of Tesco in 1993 was only about one third of Marks & Spencer, and a half of Sainsbury's, two competitors of Tesco. However, in 1995, Tesco surpassed the two competitors and was ranked first among UK retailers, from where it never stepped down. Based on sales in 2013, even when sales of Sainsbury (£23.3 billion) and Marks & Spencer (£10 billion) were combined, it was less than half of the sales of Tesco. Defeating Asda, a UK subsidiary of Walmart, it expanded to other markets including Asia, East Europe, and the United States.

What made Tesco grow like this? In 1995, Tesco did a massive promotion of Tesco Clubcard and distributed the cards to customers. Using the card, customers could receive discounts. Getting on the cycle of customer revisit and loyalty based on the card, Tesco topped the retail market and was able to accumulate sufficient data for understanding types of customers.

The fundamental purpose of Tesco Clubcard was not simply loyalty management. Former CEO of Tesco, Terry Leahy, who has a marketing background, believed that data-based quantitative marketing is very important. In need of individual level analysis of customers due to characteristics of retail industry, Tesco tried to gain sophisticated understanding of customers by recognizing customers and collecting purchase data using Clubcards. It also performed analysis and planned marketing focusing on customers' product purchase behavior and psychology.

First, it analyzed price-sensitive items and lowered prices below competitors'. Although only 6 percent of the products at Tesco were priced lower than competitors and the remaining 94 percent were more expensive, consumers compared only the 6 percent, price sensitive products and perceived that Tesco was affordable, even though mostly in fact, it was more expensive. Moreover, only the customers who were classified as socialites (actively engaging in word-of-mouth communication) were provided with discount coupons to encourage word-of-mouth marketing.

Achieving a great success in price policy using the strategies, Tesco identified customer orientation based on brands and characteristics of products customers purchased. The company also made recommendations, organized stores to fit customer types, and conducted customized strategies for individual stores.

As a result, Tesco became established as not only the UK's largest food retailer but also the most successful retailer in the world. In the late 1990s when the dot-com boom was winding down, the data analytics ability Tesco showed was truly amazing. It dominated the market with products customers wanted and the best prices based on data analytics, like a magician pulls out things from a hat. What shed a dark shadow on Tesco with no competition in the retail market?

A Drug Called Data

The root causes of Tesco's failure can be classified into three types. First, the company put data over business. High on continuing successes, Tesco trusted data analytics too much. Although issues that could not be solved by data analytics emerged as the organization became larger, Tesco made extra efforts to avoid them.

As retail stores rapidly expanded and established their presence online in the late 2000s, essential product high-volume, low-variety production and targeted specialty stores emerged as important trends. Leading traditional retails produced private brand products only in certain product groups, maintaining relationships with vendors, whereas competitors such as Aldi and Lidl implemented vertical integration of high-volume, low-variety production by streamlining development, production, and distribution.

In the retail market, Tesco gradually lost its competitiveness as it positioned itself as neither the former nor the latter. When business environment changes, long-term decision making that can change key competencies is required. Tesco's data analytics were focused on marketing, but did not provide the solution for key competencies of company.

In general, when too much focus is there on trees only, no one steps back to watch the forest. Data is not a solution to every problem. Data is only a problem solving tool to achieve the goal of a company, and one must be prepared to dump it any time it is necessary. However, Tesco failed to shake off the temptation of the magic of data.

When there is a problem, solving the problem must be the goal, and if data comes to mind first instead of the problem itself, the company has lost direction. Solving a problem from a zero-base—this is the beginning and the end of data analytics. After becoming successful by providing good products that customers wanted at low cost, focusing on the essence of retail industry, Tesco lost its core competency as it became captivated by observing data rather than customers.

Second, the analysis focused on products instead of customers. In the retail industry, it is key to sell good products at the right price. Therefore, Tesco's primary focus was on product and price, and initially this strategy worked. It recommended appropriate products, provided new products based on customers' product orientation, and maximized revenue by estimating the best price.

However, it stayed passive in the analysis of customer orientation. Orientations of supermarket customers consist of two types: behavioral and product orientations. Behavioral orientation of a customer refers to the characteristics of the process of choosing a supermarket, comparing various products, and heading to a cashier with a product. In other words, it is the orientation that shows the principle for customers making purchases. Building a marketing strategy, and comprehensive and consistent operation including location, composition, and promotions, require understanding and insight into customers' orientation. But if too much focus is placed on product orientation rather than customers' behavior orientation, it becomes difficult to make a comprehensive marketing strategy, as perspectives become narrow and all solutions become about products.

Why did Tesco, then, focus on products? Product orientation can be made into formula mathematically and statistically, and requires no customer research (e.g., interviews, surveys). Conversely, behavioral orientation analysis is partly done with internal data, but the rest must be completed using research. After getting the results on the product orientation aspect that can be resolved with internal data only, Tesco indulged in the aspect, while being indifferent to complementing it through research activities. It wanted to create a perfect solution for everything with a magic box made up of data. Consequently, although able to fully meet customer needs for products, Tesco had a weakness in market based on customer behavior (e.g., inducing visits and purchases). In other words, Tesco focused only on product data that can be easily engineered and neglected customer behavioral data.

There is a large difference between *easy to know* and *necessary* information. Once the information necessary for problem solving has been clearly identified, efforts must be made to understand how to get the information from the data. There is no guarantee that the information we need is generated from the database. Therefore, we must conduct activities of collecting necessary data and processing and recreating them. Processing the gemstone of data to make a jewel of the information we want is our responsibility. We need to create the data that we want by focusing on customers, observing their behaviors, creating a hypothesis, and detecting their signs in a database.

Third, another reason for Tesco's failure in data analytics can be rigidity of organization shown in large corporations. Tesco, which became very large, actively expanded to overseas markets, but failed in most countries except Hungary and Malaysia. In particular, in China, a battleground for global retailers, its sales continued to fall, unlike its competitors such as Walmart and Carrefour, which did well in the market. Why did Tesco's analysis-based management not work overseas? The reason is because as companies become larger, organic operation of data analytics becomes more challenging.

When a retail corporation expands to overseas, unless it responds sensitively to local customers' needs, it is difficult to surpass local competitors, no matter how excellent the system and knowhow that it introduces are. The same goes with data analytics. Applying the customer behavior and characteristics of existing Tesco customers to the customers in other countries has a limit. Just as a single solution, however stable it is, cannot be applied to all companies, data analytics must also understood and fitted to targeted markets and customers.

Having grown into a massive and complex organization, Tesco had difficulty in flexibly adapting to the new markets and environments. Tesco has conducted marketing strategies focusing on customer orientation in the UK for a long time, and in the process, analytics became increasingly focused on loyal customers; Tesco aged along with its customers. This is completely opposite to the secret of its initial success (starting from customers and then analyzing data). Ultimately, Tesco failed because it tried to fit customers to the system.

Large organizations are stable, but have difficulty in adapting to a new environment. As the organization and the processes become rigid, communication fails in the process for data analytics to achieve results.

In the end, Tesco failed to secure a superior status against competitors overseas. Analytic competency faded away without sufficient customer data, and the company was unable to get on the track of virtuous cycle. To make matters worse, due to a lack of negotiation power with local vendors and manufacturers, Tesco could not stock stores with products and brands based on the results of data analytics or implement intended promotions and price policy.

Rigidity of organization is the issue that especially larger corporation should pay attention to. Between data analytics and actual outcomes, many obstacles exist. For core competencies of a company to materialize into outcomes, the activities to remove obstacles in the execution process are a must. It is just like breaking a wall to let water flow.

Therefore, people who can control both IT and management are essential. Data analytics organizations create conceptual and logical results. They sometimes feel uncomfortable using results in real life and try to avoid the reality. However, performance comes from the power to encompass all areas of business including IT, production, sales, and marketing. This is the aspect that the companies based especially on analytic technologies such as Tesco need to pay attention to. This is because although data analytics has a great impact when it shows its strengths, obstacles to it realizing its potential lurk everywhere.

After all, Tesco fell because it was high on data and turned a blind eye to business. Ironically, the three causes of the failure illustrate the principles of successful data analytics.

First: Goal—Solve the problem at zero-base.

Second: Tool—Make data into necessary information by actively processing it.

Third: Outcome—Remove obstacles to ensure the link to performance.

In all big data projects that I have seen, these three factors determined the success and failure. This book aims at generating core principles of data analytics through analysis of cases of success and failure of actual companies. This will provide readers with insight required for analytic competency.

CHAPTER 2

Why Did Google TV Fail?

Isaac Newton Was Wrong

In *Interstellar* (2014), a science fiction movie directed by Christopher Nolan, Einstein's theory of relativity is introduced. An expedition team takes off to find a new planet for the human race to live on. Their destination is a planet located close to a black hole, and 1 hour on the planet is equivalent to 7 years on Earth. While the father, the main character, wastes about 3 hours fighting waves in the ocean on the planet, 23 years pass by on Earth, and his daughter becomes nearly as old as him. The plot sounds like it is from a storybook.

Is it not true that time passes the same whenever and wherever, and space is also immutable for everyone? For thousands of years, we have thought this to be true. The theory that time and space is not absolute but relative can be unacceptable in light of conventional wisdom. Then, how was the theory of relativity formulated?

Before Albert Einstein's theory of relativity came out, there were a few astronomical phenomena that could not be explained by Isaac Newton's theory of gravity, and one of them was the movement of the perihelion of Mercury. According to Newton's law, the elliptical orbit of Mercury was supposed to be fixed, but the fact that the entire orbit slowly rotated was observed.

At the time, no one thought the law of gravity might be wrong. Rather, believing there might be something that we do not know, scientists created far-fetched theories to fit the law of gravity. Then in 1915, Einstein announced the theory of general relativity, which goes against Newton's law, and when scientists applied the theory of relativity to the mystery of the orbit of Mercury, it explained the phenomenon precisely.

Most scientists were content with the existing law (Newton's theory) and held on to theoretical research only. While they were stuck, the truly important core essence of the problem (the orbit rotation phenomenon) was forgotten. Solving the long-standing problem, Einstein emerged overnight from obscurity. His true greatness is that he "abandoned conventional wisdom that blocked thoughts and faced the problem objectively" rather than merely his dazzling accomplishments.

Now, let us turn back to business. As big data became a "big" thing in the industry recently, data analytics has often been initiated as senior officers of a company issue a "mandatory order" to utilize data.

"We have this valuable diverse data, and we don't want to waste it. Wouldn't it give out something big if we analyze it?"

Based on this vague idea, an order is given. "News on big data is everywhere, and others seem to be doing great things with big data. Since we're also having a tough time, wouldn't it make sense to do something with it?" These types of rebukes with pressure to do something with big data, with no instructions attached, let alone clear plans, are directed at the company's personnel.

How about small and mid-sized enterprises (SMEs)? If a small venture company makes it big with data analytics or a smartphone application, the story spreads immediately. Investors in SMEs jump onto data analytics without any clear idea. However, everyone looks at successful cases and looks away from countless cases of failures.

Most of the companies that I have seen are first concerned about what they will do with data once they begin a data analytics project. That is, they try to analyze the accuracy and amount of data and the structure of the database first, and then divide roles among teams, and only then, generate useful information from the data. They analyze data day and night by selecting numerous topics. Initially it looks like amazing information might come out, but in the end, it finishes without any results. This is because they set "data" as the starting point.

A paradigm shift is extremely difficult, whether for IT personnel or strategy personnel. What corporate problems and scientific problems have in common is that they are not formulaic. These problems cannot be solved with conventional approaches, and formulas do not work. When working on the problem of perihelion movement of Mercury,

Einstein felt no need to use Newton's law, which was dominant in the field at the time. His thought was, "Whatever method that solves the problem would do." The goal was to solve the problem, not to improve Newton's law.

The same goes for data analytics. The goal is to solve a problem, not to use data. It works as long as the problem is solved, whether data is used or not. By obsessing with data and making it a priority, we miss the problem hidden behind. Stopping the obsession with data and focusing on the problem—that is the first step of successful data analytics.

Blinded by Data Analytics

"TV meets Web, Web meets TV."

In November 2010, Google released Google TV, which uses an Android-based operating system and Chrome browser. As Google TV was equipped with full browsing functions for web contents, users were able to use various media contents by downloading apps to the TV, as in a smartphone. It allowed the use of apps such as Twitter (SNS), Napster (MP3), and Pandora (web radio) as well as video services such as YouTube and Netflix.

Google TV was designed to put the web on TV. Getting results by providing personalized advertisements based on search data on Google.com, Google was aiming to provide personalized advertisements by analyzing TV viewing data with the same technology. It was convinced that its strength in data analytics would be fully demonstrated through Google TV. Leading the Google TV project, Rishi Chandra ambitiously stated, "The web ad model will further advance the TV ad market, and if we don't do it, others will eventually do it."

However, the ambitiously launched Google TV turned out to be an apparent failure. Market was indifferent, and sales were far below expectation. Logitech had to lower the price of Google TV from $300 to $250, and again to $99. There were more returns than sold products. Why did it happen?

Experts suggest that the primary reason for Google TV's failure was Google's inability in securing premium content. Major television networks such as ABC, CBS, NBC, and Fox did not provide content. In other words, there was no attractive content to entice consumers to pur-chase Google TV. Basically, content businesses did not trust Google TV. Most of all, they felt that the growth of Google TV would encroach on the existing market, including pay television.

Although true, it is not the root cause but merely a superficial rea-son, because once the number of users increases, advertisers increase too, providing sufficient reward for content businesses. This has occurred in all other markets such as smartphone, media, and music businesses. The problem at hand is the issue of "which came first—the chicken or the egg?" To find the answer, let us take a look at why consumers did not use Google TV.

Look at Humans Instead of Data

The root cause of failure of Google TV is its approach of rational cal-culation of device use behavior only, and then applying data analytics without understanding consumer behavior. In short, it forced the logic of economy and data only while ignoring the consumer. As a result, Google TV was ignored by the public, except a handful of customers who actively accommodate technology, and eventually became stranded without get-ting on a virtual cycle of "content-ads-customer."

Having tasted success, Google lost its edge in customer perspective. Just as scientists had tried to fit the problem to the formula rather than struggling with the problem itself once they learned the greatness of the law of gravity, Google tried to fit the greatness of data analytics-based search ads to Google TV as is.

Then, what should it have done instead to make Google TV a suc-cess? Corporate strategies suggest clarifying how to demonstrate core competencies targeted at actual customers by leveraging competencies. In some ways, it was a natural progression for Google, which took control of the online ad market, to expand to the several times-larger television ad market. From the economic perspective, this also works for content businesses. However, what makes it work is to know behav-ior principles of customers who actually use television. The company must be able to provide the "reason" for customers to buy and watch Google TV.

Human Brain Operates by the Law of Inertia

As mobile phones, which used to be just a medium of communication in the past, evolved to smartphones, their information delivery function significantly increased. It took a long time just for a change from a medium of communication to that of information delivery. A change in perception happened gradually in the course of about 20 years as additional functions such as texting and Internet were added to mobiles, and the release of Apple's iPhone in the 2000s accelerated the change in perception—the era of smartphone has arrived.

The smartphone market was not made by Apple overnight. Human perception has steadily changed for a long time, and Apple just realized it. In other words, although many ideas related to mobile communication existed, such as laptop, PDA, and MP3, before the change in perception became mature, they had not been integrated into the smartphone. This is because the human brain is uncomfortable with change while, it only wants to incorporate images given by device as experience.

Then, how about television and computer? The technology to integrate television and computer was developed long ago. When a product that combined television and computer was released in the 1990s, experts predicted it would rule the market. However, the product was completely ignored by the market. This was because people did not want to use the computer they used at work at home too. In the human brain, television was registered as "rest and fun," while computer was registered as "work and information." Humans use television as a lean-back. In other words, we lean on the couch and watch television passively.

The smart television developed by Google was a product that considered user aspects tremendously unlike the simple integrated television in the past. Moreover, experts predicted that, as smartphones served as a medium between television and computer, television would become smart rapidly. However, the problem was that the human brain did not change at the same pace. Television is still perceived as a passive device and the computer an active device.

In addition, Google made the error of showcasing a huge remote control mounted with a QWERTY keyboard. The keyboard input device was introduced to promote the better utilization of the search function, the strength of Google; however, this was completely the company's point of view rather than user point of view. With the human brain unchanged, the keyboard made users psychologically uncomfortable.

Strategy First

Then, how should Google TV have approached the market? From the perspective of "evolving" technical service environment and "stationary" human behavior in use, Google TV is a market in the "introduction stage" among stages in the industrial lifecycle. In this stage, only a handful of technology enthusiasts respond to new products and serve as beta testers, instead of the general public. Therefore, it was necessary to solidify hardware and data analytics technologies steadily, monitor the market, and wait for the intensive marketing point. In addition, intuitive aspects such as user-friendly, simple remote control or features to add hybrid-type channels should have been incorporated.

Unlike Google, Apple did not jump into the smart television market. At the time, Apple was timing its market entry as it was gauging the change in consumers' perception. It was exactly the same approach as before it released the iPhone.

Compared to Google, which controlled the search market using data, Apple, which focused on user behavior while leading smartphone revolution, was able to make a more appropriate decision in its hardware sales strategy. Despite being a manufacturing company, Apple is not a technology-centered but a human-centered company, and strives not to break the trust of the existing loyal customer base. Apple is watching for the chance to enter the smart television market as it patiently waits for the market to be ready after 2016.

Google made a huge investment due to error in strategizing and could not escape massive loss. In this case, the root cause was not data analytics, but the lack of understanding of consumers and wrong market strategy. The failure of Google TV once again casts a lesson of "start from not the technology, but the problem."

Regarding the issue of making people use Google TV, Google presented its own strong analytics-based ads strategy as a solution. The cause of the failure of Google TV was because Google's mind was first occupied by analytics-based ads strategy. In other words, Google failed because it decided the answer even before it had defined the problem.

As these examples show, if a company tries to solve a problem by thinking inside a box, it faces difficulties in making a good decision due to issues such as group conformity within the organization. It was not that Google's data analytics failed technically, but Google's data analytics was not helpful at all in problem solving from a strategic decision-making standpoint. Concentrating on the problem—this is why a data technology enterprise must dump data.

CHAPTER 3

Why Do They Analyze Data?

Save Data Analytics to the Last

Have you ever used a business card app? When smartphone was booming, business card apps immediately became popular worldwide. If you take picture of the card with a smartphone, these apps scan and recognize characters on business cards, automatically inputting information such as a name, company, phone number, and e-mail address. Intrigued by this feature, initially, many people used the app to input contacts. However, by the mid-2010s, the numerous business card apps all disappeared, and only a few companies such as CamCard, Buz Reader, and World Card remain. Why did the business card apps fail?

The primary target of the business card apps is salespeople. Ordinary office workers are not the main target because they respond slowly, as well as tend to shop around. From the salespeople's point of view, card management is a life-support system. Managing numerous business cards obtained from visits to customers every day is a hard but important work. It is a major part of work to manage customers by organizing the cards in an orderly fashion. Accordingly, it was salespeople who responded to the business card apps initially.

Salespeople were very sensitive to the accuracy of card recognition more than anything else. This was because each one of the information on a business card including phone number, company, and e-mail address is extremely valuable information, and incorrect recognition is directly linked to a loss. Accordingly, from the perspective of managing important information, salespeople were willing to go through card scanning, registration procedure, and pay to a certain extent as long as accuracy was ensured. For business card apps, raising the accuracy of number and letter recognition to a high level was the key issue.

The essential process before technology development and application is customer behavior analysis. Sophistication and analysis of data are the secondary issues. Defining what customers want and the requirement level are referred to as value curves. Based on the value curves, importance of each product and service component must be defined and bottlenecks (barriers to product use) must be identified. The bottleneck in the business card apps was recognition accuracy.

There has been a fierce competition in the business card app market, which was initially created with optical character reader (OCR). Most business card app companies focused on recognizing characters accurately by increasing precision of scanning and eliminating noise. They compared standard words through analysis of character conversion data and extracted words with high conversion probability. Therefore, they raised technology to allow determination of location and calligraphy, compare with standard words, and insert words with higher accuracy, when converting each character. In other words, to enhance character recognition, the companies dedicated themselves to the development of various hardware technologies and algorithms.

However, these technologies had limitations. No matter how high accuracy becomes, it was impossible to keep errors below a certain level because of physical damage to cards and various features of cameras. Consequently, the minimum requirement that app users demanded was not met. Therefore, whenever using the apps, salespeople needed to check the results and correct the errors themselves. As these chores continued, users stopped using the apps, and it became more common to keep records manually as before.

Emergence of *Remember*

Remember, a business card app that emerged in early 2014, provides the service of entering information automatically if a picture of a card is taken with a smartphone, like other business card apps. However, unlike other apps that have been struggling, this app has been a great success. It was reported it processed 6 million cumulative business cards in late 2014, and users are increasing by over 35 percent monthly. Remember was listed as the 2015 iTune's Best New App and 2015 Google Play's App of the Year, creating a phenomenon in the business card app market.

What is the secret of success of Remember, a business card app that emerged from nowhere? It is none other than raising recognition accuracy to the level salespeople wanted. Card recognition accuracy of Remember is nearly 100 percent. Without a doubt, salespeople who had been disappointed by existing business card apps responded enthusiastically. Remember took over the market overnight through word-of-mouth among salespeople who have a strong network. How did Remember overcome the limit in recognition accuracy? What algorithms and data analytics technology were used?

Surprisingly, Remember does not use algorithm or data analytics. It is not a card-management-through-character-recognition technology but input-by-human-manually technology. Over 400 typists at Remember enter information of over 50,000 cards daily in real time. Doesn't it look an outdated, unscientific method? Certainly many IT professionals and CEOs scoffed at it initially. However, the results were there. The existing apps failed, whereas Remember is making continuous growth, attracting huge investment from leading venture capitals.

What was the difference between existing business card apps and Remember in their approach? It was not an issue of simple shift in thinking. The success of Remember was the outcome of completely focusing on the business problem. Remember endeavored to investigate customers' needs and address them. Helping salespeople's card management was the ultimate task of the company. The fact it discovered was that salespeople who meet many people generally have little time, and their labor is expensive, whereas those who can do simple labor of transcribing cards were relatively abundant in the market and their labor is inexpensive. Remember met customers' needs by connecting demand and supply. This requires no profound character recognition technology. Taking a picture with a smartphone and inputting it with low-cost labor would do it.

On a macro level, the more important issue in the current situation is to secure hegemony of the business card reader market. The business card reader market is a kind of platform market that allows social networking. Expanding network services, such as extended search, could increases the customer base. Moreover, if personalized ad service for businessmen is launched, platform war with companies such as Google, Facebook, and

Twitter is inevitable. In such a market, getting on a virtuous cycle by increasing the number of users is more important than development of perfect solution through technology advances.

To get the result, we don't have to be picky about the way. There is no need to be confined to so-called elegant data analytics or algorithms. What is important is to identify what customers need and address it. While many business card app companies were hanging on to data and spending time in accuracy-oriented algorithm improvement, Remember succeeded in addressing customers' "needs" and taking control of the market.

Don't Translate Based on Grammar

Automatic translation refers to translating natural human language to another language using a computer. Compound annual growth rate (CAGR) of the global automatic translation market during the period 2012 to 2015 was 18.1 percent, and with increasing globalization, competition to develop sophisticated translation algorithms is growing. Automatic translation systems in the past were based primarily on grammatical rules. In such a system, translation is done by searching for correspondences between the structural combination of each element (word) in the original text and a target text. Often, these translation tools were used in translating technical literature or manuals, which are accurate in grammar and clear in logical composition.

However, for conversation or literary works, translation quality could not be improved beyond a point with this technology. In particular, it is very difficult to translate spoken language and idioms because phrasal translation (paraphrasing) depending on the context is required. Unlike documented language, most of colloquial language constantly changes. Thus, experts pointed out that a clear limitation exists in algorithm-based automatic translation. Eventually, the automatic translation technology market plunged into a deep slowdown.

Goal of Translation Is to Convey Meaning

What drove the automatic translation market in the 2000s was none other than big data. It used to look impossible to meet users' needs due to obsession with the technical paradigm of "translation=grammar"; however, researchers who focused on the goal of "conveying meaning" accomplished the results of "conveying meaning" (translation) "statistically" using big data.

Excellent translations done by professionals around the world are easily available. Phrasal translation began from the idea of processing such translations and using them like collective intelligence. Google's statistics-based automatic translation service made its debut in 2007. While collecting big data, Google realized that sufficiently large number of translated texts existed. The company first used data of approximately 20 billion words used in the documents of United Nations. Specifically, it created a translation system based on patterns identified in translations made by UN professional translators. In the process of developing an automatic translation program, it abandoned grammatical rules without hesitation. Although sentence translation may be considered impossible without grammatical rules, our goal is to convey a meaning in language A to language B. In the process of translating from language A to language B, a logical flow is not important. Google translation focuses on the result of translation, that is, solely on conveying meaning accurately from a user's point of view.

Human language includes those sentences for which both grammar-base logical translation is accurate and for which statistics-based translation is accurate. Google first classified words using morphological analysis of documents into conversational or literary, and then, solved grammar with statistics. In other words, it obtained statistics based on countless word pairs with the same meaning in two languages.

First, based on statistical data, probabilities are calculated for a wide range of cases depending on connections with word before and after, or a word order, and the sentence with the highest probability is created. For more accurate translation, there has to be a large number of word pairs to generate statistics. The more the data and the more recent the translation results are, the higher the quality of translation becomes. This is the principle of collective intelligence and the best part of big data utilization. Google built a system which steadily progresses as data accumulates.

This human-centered technology allows continuous, multifaceted development. As the model improves with a focus on conveying meaning, the system can understand ambiguity of natural language, changes in accents, or even silent language, and in the future, the computer can even think based on common sense like human. As a result, it can become a personal assistant that can perform simultaneous interpretation. This is the development that cannot be accomplished with grammar-based translation technology framework.

What was the success principle of statistical translation that overcame the limitations of conventional translation? It was that successful data analytics starts from goal-oriented question. The right goal-oriented question is not "How does one improve grammatical rules?" but "How does the meaning in a language remain intact?" If developers are blinded by grammatical rules when developing an automatic translator, the tools cannot overcome limitations. As experts made every effort possible to improve the quality of translation, they got bogged down by technology and lost sight of "humanity," the most important factor. Meanwhile, the pursuit of the goal of getting a solution through the approach from a human value perspective was able to establish a new paradigm of statistical translation. Prioritizing humans over technology is the only way to successful data analytics.

Case Study: Airport Traffic Data Analytics

An airport A decided to optimize transport infrastructure for airport users and sought my consultation on how to build optimal infrastructure using big data. At the time, airport A was trying to design tight, net-like routes based on number of residents per area. However, this is an inefficient method with which waste of significant resources is expected. Although airport A requested a solution based on population density linked to economic ability using the analysis of geographic information system (GIS) data, such data was in fact unnecessary for solving the problem.

What Is the Best Data to Determine Local Airport Transportation Needs?

I first decided to investigate the routes that airport users use. Our goal was to build transportation infrastructure for those who needed to get to the airport easily. Therefore, accurately pinpointing customers who have the need was the priority. To determine the airport transportation needs, I requested communication and transportation traffic data for a specific period instead of GIS data.

1. Analysis of Communication Data
   Prior to analysis of communication data, I first identified airport users in the data. I identified those who were on board a plane (turning off mobiles when the plane took off), who were on the phone at the airport, or who were identified by nearby base stations, and regarded them as airport users and traced their residences. Considering the locations where the users were on the phone between the night and the following morning as their residences, I marked the frequency of the identified residences on a map. This is the airport transportation needs of the area. Because of the sufficiently large data, representation was very accurate.

2. Analysis of Transportation Traffic Data
   Next, I analyzed traffic data to identify inconveniences customers experienced. I first identified airport customers whose final destination was the airport, and traced locations from where they get on to the transport and marked them on a map. Even though this may not provide precise location, areas with high traffic can be estimated. Since there was variation in traffic concentration among stops, it was necessary to generate an area-level traffic index.

3. Identification of Area-level Airport Transportation Needs
   By integrating the analysis results of communication and transportation traffic data, the airport transportation needs were indicated on a map by calculating the frequency of customers boarding some mode of transport in each area.

4. Optimization of Transportation Infrastructure for Airport Users
   On each of the alternative transportation systems, simulation was conducted based on scenarios. First, an airport transportation service provision hypothesis on connecting different locations was established based on customer survey results on intention to pay fare and the required time for operation, and optimal route operation

system was proposed based on estimation of profitability of individual scenarios.

In addition, if public transportation (e.g., bus, subway) did not exist in an area, additional routes were examined or dispatch factors such as optimal dispatch time and interval, and seasonal variation in dispatch were estimated.

Before jumping to data for problem solving without a plan, we always need to ask a question: "Is data required?" In my experience, many of the cases where big data analytics was assumed necessary required a use of either only a handful of data or even no data to solve a problem. The key is to solve a problem, not to look into data.

Further Study: Google's AlphaGo Beats World Champion—What Should Humans Do?

In March 2016, Google's AI AlphaGo beat Lee Sedol, the human Go champion. Some people say it is not a big deal, since the world chess champion was beaten by computers a decade ago. However, it was one of the most surprising news to many data analysts, because Go was supposed to be the last game to be conquered by computer. The number of possible scenarios or moves in chess is 10 to the power 80, but Go has 10 to the power 170, which is not just numbers, but human thinking process.

Robot Technology

In *Her* (2013), a futuristic movie of love between a person and a robot, the main character falls in love with a female operating system (OS) based on artificial intelligence. The female OS loves the main character and meets his emotional needs, serving as more than a simple conversation partner to him. Specifically, she makes jokes based on his reactions and soothes him when he is distressed. In other words, an operating system reaches the level of controlling human emotions and giving happiness to humans, which scientists argue is not impossible.

The development of a website for shopping malls, companies, individuals, or portals, often undergoes a process of an AB test. This refers to creating two groups of customers randomly, presenting them with page A and B, and selecting a page with better responses. For instance, if page A gets good responses, another page B is created and tested against page A. Repeating the experiment several times can yield the optimal design. IT service companies such as Amazon, Ebay, and Facebook have optimized their websites into personalized shopping malls using the AB test.

The current IT technology made such a tremendous advance that once automation algorithm for robot is implemented, optimal result can be created automatically by generating virtual data and performing unlimited AB tests. This makes it unnecessary for human to stylize websites and struggle to come up with services.

Machine Learning

Machine learning is a field of artificial intelligence, and a technology to enable a computer learn and comprehend an object or a situation as humans do using data. Both robot technology and the AB test are automation technologies that utilize the concept of machine learning.

Google demonstrated the results of machine learning in 2012 through the Google Brain Project. A computer identified an image of a cat on YouTube by itself. A Google supercomputer with 16,000 central processing units learned the fact that many cat images shared on YouTube had similar characters. This fact was used in creating an algorithm which used the AB test and statistical probabilities. This algorithm was then used to recognize images of cats tens of thousands of times in a trial-and-error process, and this statistically identified the image closest to the image defined as an actual cat. The computer that used machine learning recognizes objects better than humans.

Then, does machine learning operate only using human instructions (goal)? Machine learning that finds insights into and learns a new area is also possible. For instance, even when a human does not identify the image of a cat among many images, a computer can recognize the cat. The strategy is to identify shared characteristics by clustering various data obtained with human senses without prejudice. It is as if a baby looks at the world with curiosity and understands it on his or her own. It just digitalized (data) the analog (human senses).

As demonstrated in these examples, machine learning is advancing to deep learning, analysis, and modeling of how human brain operates. The comprehensive cognitive ability of deep learning is also useful in gaining insights because, for instance, it helps finding the value that humans miss due to stereotypes (which is similar to the discovery of new age music, "natural cords", in the era of being restrained by the stereotype of classical music based on "human voice cords" in the past).

A project to raise computer's learning capacity to human level with deep learning is currently underway. If this succeeds, robots with learning will work better. In the future, due to automation technology, most jobs will be performed by robots, and many of the current human jobs will disappear.

Big Data Use is a "Problem Solving Tool"

Current automation technology has two limitations in real business. First, atypical problems constantly occur, and second, machines are unable to escape the paradigm humans set up. Therefore, to find a creative solution, machine learning cannot be used.

From a data analytics perspective, it is possible to establish an improved data analytics model through ongoing efforts and create value in more sophisticated ways; however, determining the direction of utilization at the initial point comes from human problem solving capability. Both Amazon's creating recommended product pages and personalized promotions to induce customers' purchases, and artificial intelligence OS that controls emotions necessary for human relationships require understanding human behavior principles based on human insights and creative problem solving.

Ability to be Happy

Charlie Chaplin won the third place in the Charlie Chaplin look-alike contest. Does it value Charlie Chaplin less? Of course not. Chaplin does not care about contest results. For Chaplin, he does not need to look like himself.

Humans are humans. We do not need to beat machines. We do not need to compare ourselves to machines. We do not need to compare ourselves to other people. The essential objective of humans is to be happy. In this age, the most important ability is to know myself and to know how I become happy.

In the future, the work for material wealth as in the past will gradually disappear. Furthermore, as materials become abundant, humans will learn that they don't need a lot of material. However, what is left for humans is to figure out, create, and find happiness. Learning and figuring out are different. The ability to solve an atypical puzzle is not the ability to *learn* but the ability to *figure out*, which only humans can do.

AlphaGo is not happy when it learns, but a human being is happy when he or she learns.

PART 2

Data is Human

CHAPTER 4
Think as a Customer

Company A developed a data analytics solution called purchasing power index, an estimate of the likelihood of a customer making a purchase in future. It involved predicting economic ability through analysis of customers' purchase information and demographic information, and predicting how many purchases they will make in the company's other shopping channels. It was a result of the idea that rich customers actively shop everywhere.

At first glance, it is very intriguing. Would it not raise sales significantly if we identify VIP customers using a magic box and do an intensive cross-sell promotion targeting them? The purchasing power solution made a tremendous impact on the industry and grabbed prizes of various data analytics associations at the time. Then, did the purchasing power solution actually work in real business?

Contrary to industry expectations, purchasing power index had no effect at all. The marketing based on the index was much lower in effectiveness than the company's traditional VIP marketing. The solution lost its credibility in the field and was eventually abandoned by companies. Consequently, the attempt to determine customers' purchasing power with data analytics ended in a fiasco. What was the reason for the failure of purchasing power index analytics?

The reason is simple. It failed because it did not start from customers' essential needs. For instance, it started with the idea that customers who purchase many luxury goods will also purchase more online, which measures customers' purchasing power and attempts cross-selling online; however, purchasing power and purchase needs are clearly different. Simply assuming that the rich will spend money everywhere is a very naïve

idea and completely untrue based on observation of human purchase behavior. A purchase is happens only when there is a need.

A Part-time Employee of a Convenience Store Buys High-end Sneakers

Although it is true that customers with high economic ability have high
purchasing power, it is an absolute mistake to take it as needs and utilize it. For instance, even a person who enjoys luxury shopping while
being treated as a VIP at department stores may shop frugally online, and
conversely, many enjoy luxury shopping online while mostly shopping
discount products from regular stores. Thus, it is most important to know
customer orientation and shopping patterns. This is because customers
vary in the primary area of consumption depending on their orientations.

If a customer often uses a specific shopping mall, there is a reason.
Conversely, if a customer does not make a purchase at a specific shopping
mall despite being rich, it also has a reason. Why? We must identify a
customer's needs along with specific reasons for such behaviors. We must
first find the reason and understand the mechanism from the customer's
perspective. Then, we should clearly define a strategy to find a solution
and utilize data, which is referred to as hypothesis approach in consulting.

However, most companies try data first. Extracting data in this and
that way, they wish for decent insights to surface. Then they begin modeling based on vague ideas such as, "Since they have so much money,
they would buy a lot from any shopping mall." Once the IT department
provides the analysis results and statistics, those in the field use necessary
information at their discretion, hoping the value is delivered to customers
anyway.

This approach is an IT-centered approach. It is to present information easy to extract from data and let it run its course, as if wishing for

Data analytics that fails

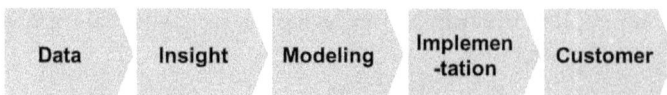

Data → Insight → Modeling → Implemen-tation → Customer

a fortune to be struck. Without a doubt, it is an inefficient process, and those in the field complain, "There is no useful information." The gap between the IT perspective, "Since I got this much done, they would be able to use it themselves," and the perspective of those in the field, "This is nothing more than impractical ideas," does not narrow down no matter what. After all, because it starts from IT instead of planning and marketing (customer), it is bound to face its limits, and of course it does not produce results.

Data Analytics Is Similar to Solving Mathematics Problems

The best way for a student to fail in mathematics is to solve problems "in the order described in the answer." The answer section details the process to insert numbers in the equation and get a solution step by step. Students who are trained to solve problems in this order always begin from "number" and "equation." However, these students are unable to solve problems in actual tests. They cannot find answers because they get lost as their heads become full of different numbers (data) and equations (tool).

The order to solve a math problem is the exact opposite. Solving a math problem starts from a deliberation, "How does one get an answer?" Then it proceeds to establish a logical process and select the necessary equations. Finally, students insert numbers in the equation to solve the problem. No matter how many numbers and equations are, there is no reason to use them all. It just requires selecting necessary numbers and equations to solve the problem. (Can you see the difference?)

The order for math is the same as the order for data analytics. Starting from data just makes it complicated and yields no result. Starting from the answer (outcome), companies can identify customers' needs,

Math problem solving

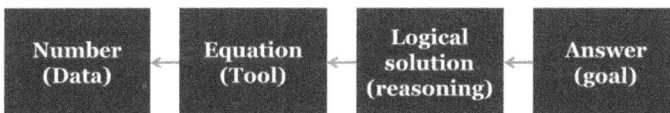

Number (Data)	←	Equation (Tool)	←	Logical solution (reasoning)	←	Answer (goal)

Data analytics principle

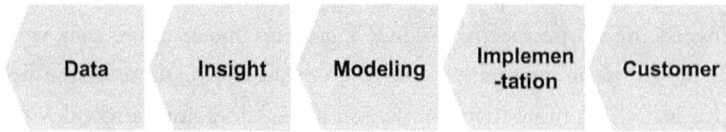

| Data | Insight | Modeling | Implemen-tation | Customer |

then, learn which data to use to solve a problem. Start from the needs of customers and those in the field, followed by processing and utilizing data.

To learn customers' needs, role playing simulation, which requires thinking as actual customers, needs to be performed. It is to live the life of customers, starting from the question of the reason to come to a shopping mall to the reason to buy, from a customers' perspective. An accurate understanding is required about what their days are like, what kind of thoughts they have and decision making they undergo when purchasing a product, and "what makes them use or not use our shopping mall when making a purchase," which is a key point. This requires observations, interviews, and research, which cannot be done with data.

Only then, plans that can be implemented in the field, such as sales and marketing, can be created and modeled. This involves deliberating to find methods to give customers the value and establishing data analytics strategies that consider data level.

Data is used only for testing hypothesis and elaborating the model at the end. The necessary data in the "big" data at the end is less than 1 percent. Data analytics is the convergent field of IT and business. Unless first the direction from customer-centered business perspective is established and the ways to meet customer needs using data analytics is presented, failure is bound to happen.

Blue Ocean Strategy of Insurance Company

Let us take a look at another case. Insurance company B was undergoing serious revenue stagnation. To address this, the IT department provided a strategy. It identified a strategic area to focus sales resources on by analyzing characteristics of the company's insurance plans and customer statistics. Based on the analysis results, an area in a small city was selected.

"The area generates lower revenues than the company average, and many residents are at an age similar to the company's main customers; therefore, if we increase the sales to the average level of other areas, sales of the company will surge." At first glance, it sounds fine. It appears that sales will increase significantly without special efforts if they do as well as other areas. The company immediately set up a plan to increase sales considerably by concentrating marketing resources to the area. They were fully prepared, by developing products with better conditions than their competitors.

However, even after conducting intensive marketing in the area for months, sales showed no sign of improvement. The sales were far below the expectations. What was the problem?

I explained that the strategy of the insurance company was unrealistic. The strategy was not based on customers' insurance product needs. Although the company intended to obtain great outcome from a blue ocean, it was not the customers' point of view. A priority is to deliberate on why customers do not buy their products from the customers' perspective.

Rather than the question, "What's the best way to increase sales in the area?", questions such as, "Who are the customers in the area? Why have sales been less? Were sales less because of less efforts were made than in other areas? What are customers' behavioral characteristics? Would sales increase by simply concentrating resources?", should have been asked first.

Financial products are sales-oriented products; therefore, it is much easier to generate repeat purchases than to generate the first sale. This is because principal-agent problem applies to insurance products. Customers do not have much knowledge of difficult financial products. They understand only a few numbers absolutely necessary (e.g., insurance premium, period), and leave the rest to an insurance planner. The ratio of product value and trust follows the rule of 20:80. Customers rely on trust, and make little rational decisions. Therefore, sales become very easy with customers for whom trust has been built and psychological barriers have been removed.

However, it requires a long time to build trust. Merely establishing a brand image and providing a large input of resources does not help build trust. In particular, customers in small cities are generally conservative and tentative in accepting outsiders. The company should understand the market and customers in small cities and take a longer-term approach from a strategic point of view; however, the company's approach solely based on data analytics and economics was the cause of failure.

Platform Companies' Dilemma

"I don't know. I don't understand men."

Jessie comes home after having an argument with her boyfriend and saying she does not want to talk to him for the time being. Then, she chats with her friend, Anne, for over an hour. While providing relationship counseling to Jessie, Anne feels frustrated, because no matter how serious the chat becomes, it is still just a scratch on the surface. What Jessie needs is to talk with her boyfriend and address the misunderstanding, but she just wants to find an easy solution. As in this example, not having direct contact with the targeted person brings a great challenge to problem solving.

Online commerce companies (such as Amazon, Gilt, Zulily), which are skyrocketing in numbers, recently have a deadly shortcoming similar to the one described above. Offline stores such as department stores and supermarkets allow direct contact and communication with various customers, identifying their needs; however, online companies cannot meet with customers. Although call centers in charge of customer service get in touch with customers' voices, even they are outsourced, making it even more difficult to get in touch with customers. Therefore, the only thing employees can do is make inferences about customers.

This is the "dilemma" that online companies have in this age that requires sensitive and prompt responses to customers' needs. This is a completely different phenomenon from the past when companies directly communicated with customers, read trends, and manage by sensing customers' needs. Consequently, it became imperative to have a sophisticated understanding of customers using data. However, most online companies still understand customers in numbers from the recency, frequency, and monetary (RFM) perspectives. This occurs because they are easy to extract from data. However, it is impossible to understand customers and identify their needs using them because customers are not "digital" but "analog."

Don't See a Customer as Money

"What's the best way to sell refrigerators in the North Pole?" This is a question commonly asked in hiring interviews for sales positions. Companies expect the answer that if there are no needs, one must create needs to sell as much as possible. This was the "provider-centered" business mindset in the past. In the present age, the rules of the game have completely changed. The current age in which supply (material quantity and information) is abundant is the "consumer-centered age." Although it is good to work hard, figuring out purchase principles from a customer's perspective is a must. A company cannot survive the consumer-centered market unless it understands consumer psychology, such as why they don't use refrigerators, whether there are needs for refrigerators, what's the barrier to making purchases, etc., prior to marketing and sales.

All of the cases introduced earlier (including purchasing power index, insurance blue ocean strategy, and platform companies' dilemma) are examples of having difficulty because the companies saw customers simply as numbers. When segmenting customers, most companies that I have consulted categorize them to date, into VIP, excellent, and general customers to suit their taste. However, this is a company-centered perspective and a short-sighted approach. Companies are always under the pressure of sales and profit. As a result, they value immediately visible monetary figures rather than seeking an in-depth understanding of customers. However, numbers such as customer transaction and profitability are important to the company but not to the customer. This is a completely supplier-centered instead of consumer-centered mindset. This type of customer segmentation does not lead to understanding of customers. How can it allow understanding of customers who vary in everything except similarity in the amount of money they spend? This type of information cannot be used in marketing, and even when it is used, it cannot be successful. Instead of seeing customers as money, it is necessary to observe their behavioral principles and identify their essential needs.

All of the cases mentioned earlier are ignoring customers' needs regarding whether customers actually would make purchases. Relying on data without consideration of customers' needs is just to scratch the surface. Sales experts who work in the field know these customer needs from experience. However, those further removed from the field, as in IT and marketing, have difficulty generating customer-oriented solutions, and often conduct analysis for the sake of analysis only.

However important data are, it is not as important as people. Start from humans. The reason why the success of data analytics is difficult is because data analytics experts lack the ability to understand customers.

CHAPTER 5

Big Data – Start from Humans

In a Sherlock Holmes short story *Silver Blaze*, a murder of a racehorse trainer and a theft of a racehorse occur. Investigating the scene of the crime, Holmes asks those involved in the case, "Was there anything unusual about the night?"

All those involved answer, "There was nothing unusual that happened."
Holmes asks another question, "Then, what about the dog that night?"
Then, everyone says, "The dog was quiet."
Holmes responded, "Isn't that unusual?"

Dogs are supposed to bark and alert the family if there is an intruder, and the fact that the dog did not bark that night was certainly unusual. Holmes reached the conclusion that the crimes were committed by someone who the dog was familiar with. Holmes tested the hypothesis of intrusion from the criminal's perspective, and it was strange to him that the dog had not barked.

What Is Profiling?

The same applies to customer analysis. When one sets up a hypothesis from a customer's perspective and examines data, one can notice data critical for understanding customers. Competent big data analysts extract essential features by processing databases and create a realistic portrait of customers based on those features. That is, they pick up traces customers leave in databases and draw their faces.

This is as if a detective asks victims about a suspect's characteristics and behaviors to narrow down the scope of the investigation.

This is referred to as customer profiling. Profiling is the approach that Dunnhumby, a retail marketing consulting company, primarily use, and its primary purpose is to "understand customers' behavior principles." The customer portrayed by data is more accurate than what customers know about themselves.

The following is the case of Target, a US retailer, reported in the *New York Times*. A father of a girl studying in high school came to a Target store and complained, "How can you send a high school girl coupons for pregnant women?" A few days later, his daughter was found to be three months pregnant. What made it possible for Target to detect the high school girl's pregnancy earlier than anyone else and send coupons? Based on purchase details such as anti-stretch marks cream and specific type of underwear, Target pinpointed the customer's pregnancy and recommended related products.

What Is Clustering?

In my experience, many CEOs take the approach of premature generalization based on just one characteristic of customers. It's like, "Online customers are about price no matter what. So, it works if it's cheap." However, this approach to customer understanding is very dangerous. Human beings have different lifestyles and behavioral patterns. Although it is fine to understand shared customer characteristics, this level of understanding is possessed by most competitors in the market. Therefore, red ocean has already been formed.

But, do not try to understand every single customer thoroughly. To understand customers efficiently, we need clustering—within the scope of marketing. Having recognized that different customer types have different life patterns and purchase behavior characteristics, one can have a comprehensive perspective for understanding all customers. After that, one should decide a target and build management strategies using the subtle behavioral characteristics of the target.

Amazon announced the plan to reduce delivery time to 30 minutes. Would a 30-minute delivery be possible in a country as big as the United States? Amazon creates sales plans and manages inventory by determining consumers' needs in real time. It profiles customer orientation and examines purchase history using data analytics. In addition, it predicts purchase volumes for each product based on estimation of demands using regression analysis of customer purchase cycles and purchase trend data. Then, would it be possible to predict individual customer's purchase volume? It would be meaningless to predict individual volumes using statistical analysis due to the large margin of error; however, predicting for area groups is definitely possible. It cannot be predicted how many apples a customer would buy this month, but it can be predicted within a very small margin of error how many apples 1,000 customers in an area would buy.

Clustering enhances big data use. We can see customer type collectively and insightfully.

Data analytics is performed by creating hypotheses for a few customer types and profiling through statistical clustering to create groups of customers based on similarity. Understanding behavior of each customer type and marketing based on this understanding can result in the best outcomes.

1. Profiling could be simple and better

    The case that I introduce now to explain customer profile is the project requested by a retailer that began as an online shopping mall. This company launched an offline business as it had been successful in online business; but to its surprise, its offline stores were struggling. The plan was simply to increase new VIP customers by coaxing its online customers to use offline stores. But, the problem was how to target customers and to avoid wasting money by conducting large-scale promotions excessively.

    Therefore, I concluded that it was necessary to understand customers through profiling shopping mall customers, screening the customers who have potential to become offline VIP customers, and enticing them through customized promotion.

    Profiling is to index behavior characteristics based on customer needs. It has the following six stages.

    Stage 1 Defining Attribute Types

    First, hypothetical customer types are established and attributes that can differentiate various customer groups are defined. Based on basic research, customer interview, and brainstorming, hypothetical clusters of customers and their respective characteristics are generated for typology.

In the said project, the hypothetical customer groups included "window shopping impulsive buyer," "accessory maniac," "discount seeking buyer," and "value seeker." Then, attributes that can differentiate the groups were identified and classified into the following main behavior types and attributes: (1) shopping mall visit behavior (why visit?), (2) purchase behavior (why purchase?), (3) product orientation (what orientation in purchase?), and (4) product group type (buy what usually?).

Stage 2-1 Defining Behavior Attributes

After defining attribute types, to index each type of customer, behavior attributes are defined by designating attributes that have distinct characteristics and can be extracted from data.

For instance, in the case of the shopping-at-work type, the online access time is constant as lunch hours or afternoon. The impulse-buyer type has high frequency of page views and long stay on the site. These attribute types show distinct characteristics of the customer and can be extracted from data.

Stage 2-2 Indexing Behavior Attributes and Applying Profiling

The attributes generated from the process are then indexed. Each attribute can have more than one basis. For instance, if defining the impulse-buyer type with a single basis of a large number of page views, one could be misled. Therefore, to reduce such errors, a variety of basis is identified, including login frequency, proportion of fashion product purchase, and brand concentration. Attributes are indexed by applying weights to these basis and adding up the scores.

Stage 3-1 Defining Product Attributes

Customer profiling must also be used to define product attributes. This refers to determine what each product means to customers in order to analyze product orientation. That is, the individual products purchased reveal customers' orientations, and product attributes specify these orientations and assign an orientation score to each product.

For instance, product attributes can be defined as "popular and mass appeal," "adventurous and appealing to maniacs," and "luxurious and expensive." These product attributes also need to have distinct characteristics and be extractable from data.

Stage 3-2 Indexing Product Attributes and Applying Profiling

As with behavior attributes, product attributes are also indexed. For instance, the popular-and-mass-appeal product attribute is indexed based on market share in its product group, and the trendy-product orientation is indexed based on growth rate.

Then, this is applied to profiling, which is accomplished by multiplying a purchase quantity of product of interest by attribute index of the product. To illustrate, when calculating the trendy-product index of a customer, if the customer purchases one product with index of 100 percent and two products with indexes of 50 percent, the trendy-product index is (100% × 1 + 50% × 2) / 3 = 66.7%.

We can also measure customers' shopping age (not real age), which shows how young or old customers spend. Since real age does not fully show customers' shopping propensity, shopping age is more accurate. After measuring the mean age of each product, average age is calculated from the products a customer buys (statistical standardization needed). Shopping gender can be calculated in the same way.

Stage 4 Completing Customer Profiling

Customer profiling is completed by combining behavior profiling and product profiling described earlier. The result of this profiling is used in understanding of individual customers and targeted marketing in the future.

2. Clustering

Understanding customers from a macroscopic perspective requires clustering customers based on behavioral characteristics. The reason for it is, first, because knowing customers with data only has limitations. What data shows about customers is only a very small part of them. If we try to understand everything with results of profiling, bias may occur. However, if we cluster them, similar customers are grouped together, and as a result, big data effects emerge, allowing increasingly sophisticated understanding of customers.

Second, clustering is required because it is difficult to conduct promotion targeting a great number of customers. Although understanding of how customers move around is required in the planning stage of marketing, customers must be clustered into meaningful categories when targeting in blocks for activities such as sending texts or e-mails and conducting mass marketing.

In this project, clustering was done using the results of profiling discussed earlier by using statistical clustering, which standardizes profile results and groups customers with similar orientations. Once clustering was completed by determining the number of optimal clusters, a persona was defined for each cluster.

To be specific, first, customer clusters were understood with average index and demographic information of individual clusters. Second, a sample of customers representative of each cluster were selected and interviewed. Through additional research, persona of each customer cluster was clearly defined. Understanding of customer behavior principles is achieved through role playing simulations.

3. Find Customer's Pain Point

"Your efforts will never betray you."

In general, the marketing department takes on a lot of work. They try to do all different types of marketing and endeavor to do every single task that faces them. However, implementation is often delayed and work is carried out frequently in a disorganized manner. When the direction for marketing is not clearly set, personnel are not convinced of their work. Marketing must be preceded by strategy building. However complicated a situation looks, a cause can be identified if deliberating step by step based on a framework and the cause must be resolved. In the following, the framework for customer purchase stages is discussed.

All customers undergo a series of formalized process in acquiring products and services they need. This process consists of three stages: "awareness of purchase needs → collection of available options → decision." In this process, customers never skip a stage, nor perform more than one stage at one time. The importance of each stage varies across customers and products.

Therefore, if a purchase does not occur, the stage at which it got stuck needs to be determined and a root cause identified. The root cause is called customer's *pain point*, and what requires most attention is to clearly define customer's pain point and organize strategies and programs to solve it. Although certain parts can be quantified using customer profiles and cluster types, efforts to deliberate while simulating cluster-specific customer behaviors in stages using the persona designated earlier are needed.

The first stage of the product and service purchase process is awareness of purchase needs. As human senses are limited, customers are often unaware of purchase needs despite the existence of useful products. They easily experience purchase needs when necessities they use frequently (e.g., soaps, socks, milk) are out, but for the product needs that occur sporadically (e.g., musical instrument for hobby, gourmet food, fashion products), they don't. Therefore, in the latter case, customers need to be frequently exposed to products, so that they experience needs of "wanting to buy."

In addition, there are customers who are easily aware of purchase needs, while others are not. Some customers are opinionated enough to buy only the products they want to buy, and for other customers, exposure to product information and browsing products leads to purchase. In the latter case, providing a product catalog or new product information can generate a greater effect than in the former case.

In the second stage of collection of available options, customers become ready to make a final decision by comparing many choices of the product that they need to buy. Once they have a product to buy, they compare two to five products depending on the importance of the product and their orientations.

For instance, if purchasing a smartphone, they compare at least products of three companies—Apple, Samsung, and Motorola. It is extremely rare to make a purchase after learning about a product of just one brand, and customers delay purchase decision if they are not convinced that they've checked and compared all available options.

Therefore, in the case of shopping malls, it is necessary to show target customers all available options to reassure them. Shopping malls must have a variety according to customers to allow them to compare products easily. When failing to convince them 100 percent, it is possible to help customers skip the stage of collection of available options using offers such as time sale or limited offers.

In the third stage of decision, customers make a choice among collected available options based on their preferences. First, they compare key attributes (i.e., design, price, brand, function, quality), then, they calculate the weighted average to suit their taste in their mind. The attributes and importance considered in the process vary across customers. To some customers, price, and to other customers, specific functions are important. As this is shown in customers' purchase orientation profile, purchase decisions are induced using price offers or recommendations for personalized feature based on the purchase orientation.

4. Recommending Like Amazon

Many companies recommend products to customers based on superficial data only. Would shoes recommendation marketing be effective to customers who buy the brand of the company every time? "Since he bought shoes last time, he would buy shoes next time too." Of course, it would high for the customer to buy shoes. However, what is the use of making an offer for the same product to the customer who regularly buys the product? Not only other products are not sold, but also there is a drawback of over-promoting the product that would be purchased anyway. The purpose of retail marketing is to induce more product purchase by identifying customers' various needs.

Therefore, effective product recommendation strategies are mainly recommending products associated with two perspectives: individual and cluster.

Individual association is the calculation method primarily used in associated product recommendations on Amazon and eBay. Using the extent different customers buy the products in common, associated product is identified by multiplying the proportion of the same products purchased by different customers. For example, association between product A and product B is equal to the proportion the customer who bought product A bought product B x the proportion the customer who bought product B bought product A [n(A∩B)/ (n(A)*n(B))]. Therefore, association of one product with all other products is obtained. If there are N products, N × (N – 1) association data are generated. This is basic concept of association rule extended to many high-tech derivations nowadays.

Once association between products is calculated, associated product scores and ranks are obtained by multiplying the number of purchases made by an individual by association between products. The individual association recommendation here is to recommend the product and the brand ranked high in association. (In this book, association is calculated simply using the square root function. In reality, various statistical techniques are used.)

However, there is a limit in simply recommending purchase and viewing associated products, because product assortment is impossible unless sufficient data is accumulated. Customer type clustering data is required to complement this. Clustered data is particularly useful when targeting new customers, which is to recommend cluster associated products by making inference on customer types and clusters using basic information of customers.

While the purchase product associated recommendation discussed above induces re-sell or up-sell, cluster associated product recommendation is strongly aimed at inducing cross-sell. When people with similar behavior types and product orientation are grouped together, products they want to buy are also similar. In the case of new customers, the strategy is that like-clusters are generated as much as possible using individual characteristics (including demographic data), and using the clusters, product sets that each cluster primarily purchased are recommended.

Platform-oriented companies need to optimize the composition to encourage customers to continue visiting. Once individual-specific recommended products are identified using the strategies described above, user interface (UI) is created in such a way that allows them to catch customers' eyes. Companies induce steady visits and utilization by organizing recommended product list for each specific section to be seen at a glance as in YouTube and Amazon, and using the logic that checks intention while keeping changing recommended friends as in Facebook.

5. Pilot as Quick-win

In this project, to verify data analytics, I decided to implement offline growth strategy, which was originally intended.

First, 50,000 potential offline VIP customers were selected based on cluster channel purchasing power among online customer groups. By adding more selection criteria, major target group was designated as the group of customers who have short stay time, lower number of page views, high level of interest in fashion products, and live close to the offline store of the company.

The interview results showed that the customer group usually made a lot of offline purchases except special cases, and data verification results showed that they had the highest level of offline purchase. In the customer group, the customers without purchase experience in the offline store of interest were designated as the primary target. The designation was based on the consideration that they have offline needs according to the characteristics of the customer cluster but aren't aware of the offline store; therefore, recognition marketing would have the highest cross-sell effect.

The results of sending SMSs and e-mails for information delivery to this customer group showed that customers began visiting the store and making purchases when they were reminded about the offline store 2.4 times on an average. Remarkable difference was found including increase in purchase response rate by over 60 percent compared to the conventional approach. Later, as data was accumulated, we made the model more elaborate by changing weights of attributes based on results of regression analysis with the growing database. As a result, a self-improving system, in which accuracy of recommendations and offers increase as data accumulates, was established.

6. Surround Customers with Omni-Channel

Omni-channel strategy is implemented to create a synergy effect among channels by the company that owns multiple sales channels (offline channels such as department stores, street shops, outlets, duty free shops, supermarkets, shopping mall complexes, and online channels such as web and mobile).

In my experience, most companies try to create an omni-channel strategy from a simple idea such as this:

"Wouldn't it sell more if we guide department store customers to shop online? I have a hunch that if we get online customers to our stores near their homes, additional purchases would be made."

I always advise that this type of thinking is dangerous. This is because it misses the process of deliberating on the actual purchase principle from a customer's perspective. An approach that misses logical explanation of why a customer buys is bound to end fruitless.

Illusion of Omni-Channel

Let us take the case of Gap, a global clothing company, implementing omni-channel strategy as an example. Since June 2013, Gap has provided services that allows customers to pick up the products they reserve online at offline stores. As a result, Gap's online sales in April 2014 increased by 21.5 percent compared to that of previous sales. Gap evaluated this strategy that allows offline picking up of products purchased online a successful case of synergy. But, is it really a success of omni-channel strategy?

The online shopping mall market is a high-growth market, and all companies report 10 to 20 percent growth annually. There is no evidence that the omni-channel strategy led to online growth. It was the case of the customers who were going to buy offline anyway making online purchases. If cross-sell between channels increased and led to sales increase as the company intended, both online and offline sales would have increased, but this was not the case. In fact, during this period, online and offline sales of Gap grew only at 3.2 percent, which is considered a stagnation considering inflation. Then, is omni-channel really an illusion?

The omni-channel strategy does not always fail. But for it to be successful, the role of omni-channel must be clearly defined and its nature must be clarified as explained below. Many CEOs have a vague understanding of omni-channel as "removing the barrier between online and offline to make customers use channels more."

Omni-channel increases synergy among channels in three ways: (1) by utilization of transportation channel, (2) by showrooming solution, and (3) by cross-sell between channels.

Transportation channel utilization is the use of current offline stores as one mode of transportation for the online channel. Showrooming solution is increasing sales by providing opportunities and information to customers who browse online and buy offline or who browse offline and buy online. Cross-selling between channels is inducing additional sales by recommending more appropriate channel based on identification of customer needs.

Among them, cross-sell between channels is most effective, because it is directly linked to meeting customer needs and revenue generation. Based on my experience, only the customers with low profitability respond to transportation channel utilization, and as many customers already meet their needs well, showrooming solution is hardly effective.

The case of Gap is the case of using offline stores as transportation channel. It does not affect the total revenue significantly because it is different from the highly effective cross-sell between channels. Although offline stores may play a role of a transportation channel to an extent, the effect is less than large.

The true effect of omni-channel depends on whether it meets customer needs. Companies must think from actual customer perspective. In the case of Gap, would online customers want to make efforts to come to a store and pick up a product? Would it be easier to get it shipped and delivered? Few customers would make extra efforts to visit stores to save shipping cost, and it would be unlikely for them to make additional purchases. Moreover, if online is cheaper, only the showrooming cherry-pickers who browse offline and buy on mobiles or web will increase, making offline stores useless.

Omni-channel transportation synergy strategy can be effective when large retail companies such as Amazon use local bases such as convenience stores as distribution centers. Use by ordinary clothing company has very limited effect (surely loss is small even when it fails).

Target Customers' Channel Needs

Implementing a growth-oriented, omni-channel strategy requires focusing on cross-sell between channels which begins from understanding customers. The primary task is to deliberate on why customers buy offline or why they buy online.

If a company requests for a consultation, expressing a wish to move offline customers online, I ask, "Why should customers come online?" The answer is the same as the case of the insurance company examined earlier. "We want to secure a customer base in the area in the small city because no one there use our insurance." But it is just the company's wish, reflecting nothing from the perspective of the customer. There must be a reason for customers in the area to not use the company's insurance. Finding the reason is the first task. In the same manner, there is a clear reason for offline customers not wanting to come online.

Utilize Omni-Channel Strategy Tailored to Customer

Customers always have reasons to use a specific shopping channel. These reasons may include: "I can shop from home comfortably," or, "It's cheaper, and it doesn't take long," etc. Reasons for offline customers include: "The department store near home or where I go to often has brands that I want," or "I know the store owner," or "I don't feel comfortable unless I wear them before I buy, and I don't know about online shopping malls." In addition, three are product group preferences for specific channels, such as a tendency to buy cosmetics online and clothing offline.

These show that customers have goals for specific shopping channels in their mind, and their own ways of use. Once customers' channel needs are identified, companies must meet the needs. In other words, companies identify offline customers who have needs for advantages of online stores and provide the advantage (e.g., discount, easy buy), to raise additional online sales. The same applies to cross-sell on offline for online customers. Suggesting wearing offline or informing them of offline stores near home also meet their needs. To summarize, omni-channel strategy must be planned to fit the convenience of the customer instead of the convenience of the company.

Implementing omni-channel cross-sell target marketing requires data analytics and utilization. Data analytics method for the process is as follows. First, customers are clustered by generating hypothetical customer types and processing data to differentiate the types. Then, characteristics of each customer cluster are determined, and key needs are understood. The individual customer types have channel-specific purchasing power (channel potential), which will be discussed in detail in the following.

Channel Potential

Channel potential refers to the likelihood for a customer to increase sale in a channel of interest. As customers' behavior, orientation, and economic ability are similar within a cluster, preference of the channel is also similar. In such a case, customers who currently make small purchases compared to their channel preference are likely to be VIP customers.

This is referred to as the principle of regression to mean, and for instance, if the amount of monthly mobile purchase of cluster A is $500 and the amount of monthly mobile purchase of cluster B is $200, customers in cluster A are more likely to increase mobile purchase than those in cluster B, if both have the same $300 monthly mobile purchase amount. As shown here, the customer group with higher channel potential (i.e., easier to cross-sell between channels) is identified, and the channel they have needs for are promoted intensively. Use of this approach can achieve considerable revenue growth at minimum cost.

Another misunderstanding CEOs have of omni-channel strategy is that it results in cannibalization. They think that if good customers who buy a variety of products offline are moved online, only low-cost products are sold and in turn, if sending offline discount coupons to opportunistic online customers, it is possible for them to act like cherry pickers and profitability of the company will suffer; however, this is just unfounded concern.

Based on my experience, when a shopping channel is added, total consumption (sum of online and offline) increases by 21 percent. Human shopping amount depends on their wallet. When customers are given more shopping channels, the added channels generate purchases, and although purchases may slightly decrease in existing channels, more consumption occurs in terms of the sum of online and offline. In other words, sales of the competitor decrease. In conclusion, instead of worrying too much about cannibalization, companies must identify shopping channels customers have needs for using a sophisticated approach and actively seek channel cross-sell.

Showroom Mix

One of the e-commerce trends is the offline launch of online shopping malls. What is the reason for large online shopping malls such as Amazon launching department stores or road shops? This is because customers have some showroom needs despite online stores. Gradually, customers use showrooms offline and purchase online.

The ratio between offline and online vary according to the change in IT technology and human perception. According to the analysis results of Value Management Group, the proportion of online purchases in all purchases was below 20 percent in the mid-2010s, but it is predicted to increase to about 60 percent by 2020. Eventually, only the stores used as showrooms will remain offline, and personalized or targeted independent shopping malls that meet various customer needs will increase online.

To find an optimal ratio between online and offline stores, the current online and offline ratio based on showrooming needs must be identified and stores for showroom purposes must be arranged on the way customers move. Shopping malls targeting teenagers do not currently require many offline stores as compared to online shopping malls targeting older customers, which require a certain number of offline showrooms.

CHAPTER 6

Why Does Nike Compete with Nintendo?

"Nike's greatest competition is Nintendo."

As its growth rate slowed down, Nike, the world's No. 1 sports product company in the past, designated companies like Nintendo, Sony, and Apple as new competitors. Why? Studying its customers' behavior with spare time, Nike found that it fell behind in the competition as its customers favored easy exciting video games or entertainment in recent years. Nike defined its competitors for customers' spare time from a customer's perspective.

In the current platform business, occupying customers' spare time, which is not much, translates to the revenue of the future. In that context, Nike needed to occupy customers' spare time. (Monetization was an issue for later.) Nike secured customers' time by sponsoring various sports activities to draw people's attention. In particular, it focused on occupying time by promoting sports activities (futsal or extreme sports) popular among young people who enjoy video games. In the process, Nike built trust by putting forward the brand at the forefront and conveyed a strong sports image through ongoing exposure.

This made customers who watch and enjoy sports start developing positive feelings toward the Nike brand unconsciously, and they gradually became loyal customers. Eventually, Nike was able to harvest the fruit of customers' spending in the long term. Once a company captures customers' eyes and ears along with their time, it becomes easy to generate revenue. It is of utmost importance to take customers' time (which is traffic, in other words).

New Buzz Life

How can taking customers' time be applied to technology-based platform companies? BuzzFeed, a news and entertainment website founded in 2006, had the company value assessed around $850 million in 2014. This is over three times the amount for which Amazon purchased the *Washington Post* in 2013. This shows how high the future value of BuzzFeed was assessed in the market, and the key reason is none other than traffic.

The lower quality journalism consisting of light humor called "clickbaits" became popular among young users on SNS. BuzzFeed created sophisticated content sets, targeting the young customer base. The primary weapon of BuzzFeed was the technology to identify the information appropriate for target customers and place it at the right place. The biggest goal was to make users "visit and enjoy" based on the strategy.

The core technology of BuzzFeed is based on data analytics. The process begins with creating the content likely to attract readers' attention based on analysis, which is then clicked by customers for an article or an advertisement. It is noteworthy that it provides content tailored to individual customers and customer types by optimizing even design, headlines, and articles through collaboration among marketing personnel, engineers, and designers. It makes users visit the site no matter what by creating the "playground of their own."

The users who were thrilled about this service spread the word everywhere on the Internet, and the word reached even the older generations. Various customer segments have begun enjoying social news and gradually used higher quality news, statistics, and personalized services.

Bait Customers with "Data"

Ironically, conventional newspapers such as the *New York Times* and *Washington Post*, which lost market leadership to BuzzFeed, grew in the same way in the beginning. They began as companies that provided news scrap service. Specifically, they reviewed the contents of tens of newspapers, selected important articles, and processed them into more readable format by hiring writers. To draw attention, they even used sensational headlines such as "100 most influential people in the world" (similar to "41 people you won't believe actually exist"). In other words, what they did was just to adapt content from a customer's point of view.

To summarize this process, first, they place content anyone would respond to at the front. Then, to encourage customers to keep visiting, they identify customers' needs and keep developing and providing customized content. Then, they establish a sustainable growth model through a virtuous cycle for monetization such as advertisements and services.

Visit → Revisit → Monetize

This is a basic principle of business-to-consumer (B2C) market as well as distinct characteristic of the current digital media that are spreading through primarily SNS and mobile, such as the *Huffington Post* and the *NewsPeppermint* in addition to *BuzzFeed*. A point to keep in mind here is that the foundation is always the customer. Customer traffic is equal to the value of a company. In this era, only the companies that have customer contact points survive.

Global Chicken Game

The consumer goods manufacturing industry is currently in an impasse. The reason behind it is that unlike in the past when manufacturers distributed their products directly to customers through stores they owned, large retail stores such as Walmart and Amazon have monopolized retail business and taken control of customer contact points. This has led to many manufacturers losing market leadership and power.

In the entertainment content market of the past, telecommunication companies used to own their own content service platforms such as music and games. However, as IT companies took over customer contact points using smartphones and OS, telecommunication companies had to give most of their profits up to the IT companies.

Among delivery apps (e.g., Door Dash), which have become popular recently, the competition for customer contact platform is also fierce. This market is making an impact as they bring together customer contact points that individual restaurants used to manage themselves. From a customer's point of view, this is convenient since restaurant information is assembled in one place. However, it is inevitable for total revenue of restaurants to fall.

In the case of the financial industry, loan agents and general agency (independent insurance agencies) firmly hold customer contact points, intruding on domains of banks and insurance companies respectively. Large customer contact companies such as Amazon are attempting to enter the financial market through payment services. As this customer contact point competition intensifies, conventional financial companies will serve only as product developers or providers of infrastructure.

The essence of data analytics in this era is the human being, that is, the customer. In this age of oversupply, negotiation power of the purchaser and the customer's decision power increases, whereas the supplier's power diminishes. To make matters worse, competition and the threat of alternatives are increasing.

The areas removed from consumers, such as manufacturing or production of services, have more standardization and are easier to imitate. As information supply grows, technology is standardized, and as automation and machine learning technology advance, further enhancement of productivity is difficult to expect. Eventually, cost saving through simplification and upsizing of production process are left as the only option.

Customer contact platform

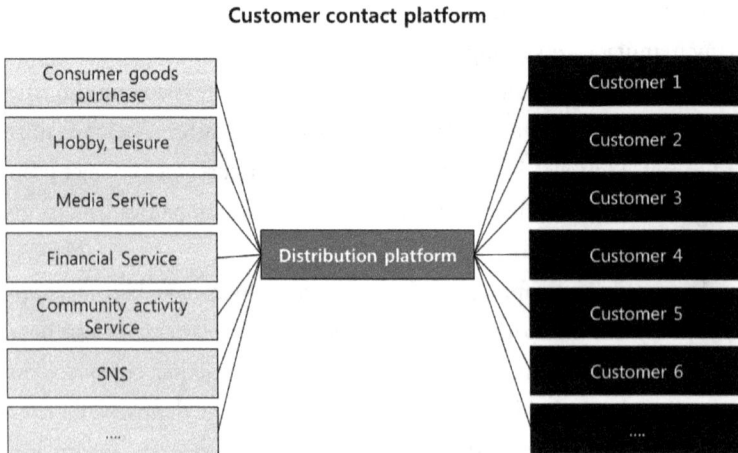

Therefore, in this day and age, large manufacturing companies based on secondary industry in the past reach a plateau, and their importance in the industry becomes less.

Companies that are growing now are mostly knowledge-based service enterprises. In particular, what all global service enterprises have in common is that they provide customer contact point services. Specifically, they secure a large customer base established with platforms based on specific services, followed by the winner-takes-it-all approach for profits. To summarize, the growing companies secure customer contact points first and raise enormous revenues by exercising monopoly in the industry.

Case Study 1
Poker Player Who Utilized Big Data Algorithm

In 2015, a big data research institute in the United States requested me for a software algorithm for the poker game called *Texas Holdem*. The institute wanted to apply the analytic technology for data-based customer psychology used in marketing instead of merely developing an algorithm.

How does poker relate to customer psychology analysis? Poker is not a game of logic but of psychology. This is consistent with marketing, which studies human psychology. I proposed to use a machine learning scheme to the algorithm by analyzing types of opponents.

In 1997, Deep Blue, IBM's supercomputer, shocked the world by defeating a world chess champion. The software plays the game by searching a database of past chess games and chooses a move which has a higher probability of succeeding. In other words, it is a simple principle that the more accumulated chess game data, and the faster the computer's computation, the higher the probability to win. In a chess game, the number of moves in a game reaches 10 to the power 80. Thus, in a chess game, it is impossible for a human to win against computer.

Then, would a computer also win in a poker game? Software developers attempted development of a poker game using a chess algorithm. However, even until now, with computer performance progressing a hundred fold, most attempts have ended as failures. What is the reason?

Visible and Absolute Chess versus Internal and Relative Poker

Poker is psychological warfare. In poker, the players do not know the other players' hands, and if a hand is not good, the player may fold. One may bluff by betting high even with a not-so-great hand. It is a psychological game that does not allow for analysis with visible information. While a probability of win can be quantified with a single logic in chess, poker requires applying logic completely differently, depending on the orientation of the opponent. Poker is the game that can never be won without analysis of opponents' psychological pattern.

Would It Be Solved by Machine Learning by a Supercomputer?

Professor Michael Bowling's research team at the University of Alberta in Canada created an enormous poker database as they conducted poker games 24 trillion times a second for 69 days. The number of games was greater than the number of all the games that the human race has ever played. Would the supercomputer with the gigantic database be able to win against a human? In conclusion, simply improving the hardware performance of a computer and increasing the amount of data have all failed. This is because they lacked the aspect of considering opponents' psychological patterns.

Behavioral Types from a Poker Player's Perspective

I concentrated research in clustering opponents' behavioral patterns into types and implementing algorithms for each type. The type here refers to the type of "opponent's response to me." The opponents play the game as they observe my behavior. This is why others' perspectives inevitably come in. I classified poker players' significant response types (brain operation process) hypothetically by collecting and reviewing various games.

Once displayed cards and my cards have been set up, opponents' response patterns were collected and their types were determined. A significant amount of information can be obtained from even a single game, because with every deal, data on changes in displayed cards, "my response", and opponents' response collectively provide basic information to understand opponents. At the beginning, we play by certain rules, which are called policy (pattern of general player rule). Specific types of response patterns were identified by performing regression analysis on the data of a certain number of initial games, and winning algorithm is performed once data is below a certain level of error.

Winning Algorithm

First, depending on the situation, opponents' cards and responses are predicted. Then, the logic to win against the opponent type is applied using the strategy of combining principles and anomalies appropriately. Poker can be won in the following two ways: winning by showing the hand at the end and winning by letting opponents fold. In other words, one can choose to implement tactics to win through bending rules optimally over several games (counterploting while exposing patterns), or to acquire chips using steady pressure. Because data accumulates as dealing progresses, probability of winning steadily increases. When the type-specific algorithms were actually applied, the probability of wining was 10 percent higher than existing poker programs based on single algorithms. As it applies machine learning, the model becomes more sophisticated in type correspondence as results of actual games accumulate.

Poker programs are not difficult at all although they look complicated with the psychological aspect being applied. Developers have difficulty because they try to approach using a calculation logic only instead of a human perspective. Chess is similar to Newton's laws of motion, and poker is similar to Einstein's laws of relativity. The type of behavior at the moment a poker player plays against an opponent cannot be specified with absolute certainty. The absolute algorithm for winning the game does not exist, and the developer must think of behavioral pattern from a poker player's perspective and implement and apply algorithms by analyzing and processing data accordingly.

This perspective is identical as the approach that I took in the data analytics project. Most of the businesses in the current era require the data analytics approach from the consumer behavior psychological perspective. However, many companies continue to believe that problems will be solved with large-capacity, high-performance hardware. This is the age of material and information oversupply, and the businesses that use materials and information are the red ocean with already fierce competition. What we need to do is to understand humans and create value. This requires the fusion of humanities and technology.

True value does not come from the amount of data analytics and processing speed. As shown in the case of the poker database, computing technology has steadily advanced, and unlike in the past when only accumulated data was used, today, unlimited amount of new data can be generated. In other words, this is the era of data and an environment can be easily created for use if wanted. Now that infrastructure is at its best, there are unlimited possibilities, even with small data and a computer only instead of big data and powerful servers.

Case Study 2
Costco, the More You Buy, the Cheaper It Gets

Costco implements the strategy of reducing price for the products that sell more. It completely contradicts the fundamental principle of demand and supply in economics. However, in the ongoing recession in the retail industry, Costco made a steady growth and recorded $112.6 billion sales and $20.6 billion net profit in 2014, continuing a winning streak. What is the secret of their success?

Customer Contact Platform Business

Costco's popular products' prices are much lower than their competitors' prices. This makes their members believe all products sold at Costco are priced lower, and as a result, members' loyalty increases. Costco gains consumers' trust and sells more products by attracting more members. Thanks to this, they can reduce the price further.

Costco says that "interests of the company and interests of customers are identical." This is not incorrect, but to understand the success of Costco pricing policy properly, it is necessary to analyze its significance in business management.

Selling a few categories of products with large purchase demands is a strategic positioning for the target customer group. That is, Costco positioned themselves by targeting customers with needs for purchasing mid-quality products with mass appeal in large quantities. This means that they expanded the platform by gaining consumers' trust. In other words, Costco implemented the strategy dedicated to customer contact platform business to lock in customers.

Then, would Costco keep this policy? Probably not. This is because monetization would gradually increase. Costco basically operates based on membership. If not a member, one cannot even enter the store. Although product margins are much lower than Walmart, they cover the rest with membership fee. Therefore, once they secure customer contact points, they will surely realize monetization by raising membership fees or prices.

Would It Become Cheaper If Selling More?

Since 2000, online commerce has grown fast and large supermarkets of large corporations opened up while global SPA brands established, upsizing in retail industry has progressed rapidly. The goal of all of them was to save costs through upsizing, and through which, to provide consumers with benefits of selling at lower costs. This is the concept of the more, the cheaper, which is Costco's strategy of alignment of company-customer interests. Then, would it actually become cheaper if in bulk?

Let us take a peek at their future using the case of Amazon. Starting as an online retailer, Amazon also solidified loyal customer base by enticing customers with bait products and pricing, and providing customized services. Ultimately controlling customer contact points, Amazon is providing products and services by expanding to the areas of planning, production, and logistics. Securing the leadership in retail, Amazon is increasing revenue through vertical integration by participating directly even in production. It is monetizing by providing premium membership, manufacturing products, and gradually increasing prices.

There Is No Free Lunch

Upsizing is a global phenomenon. As economic barriers between countries are destroyed and large corporations are established in production, processing, and manufacturing, the process of upsizing is accelerated. Today, the global chicken game is an unavoidable reality. Initially, manufacturing shows upsizing, because rounding up of companies can save cost and expand the market. In the business-to-business (B2B) industry, upsizing is easy. Thus, in the future, the B2C market will show upsizing. This is the so-called upsizing in consumer gathering. This is the current picture.

In the beginning of upsizing, it looks as if costs are reduced and customers are benefited. However, from the moment the absolute majority uses the platform and barriers to entry are formed, the price goes up and consumers begin to be disadvantaged. This is because from a CEO's perspective, there is no reason to provide at low cost.

In the current era, making money is basically through the following three principles: finding a large wallet (concentrating on the richest), finding what is in high demand (entering new growth markets), and reducing supply (monopolizing). Considering each of the goods and services around humans as independent markets, the principle of making money is to share people's wallet. Once the market becomes monopolized, the price can become "as much as people are willing to pay" in the absence of price competition.

What the capitalistic system is most wary about is monopoly. Based on economics, when a market is a completely competitive system, suppliers' profits become close to zero, and consumers are benefited considerably. However, if a monopoly is formed in the market, companies use all possible means to generate maximum profits. In the situation with no alternative, consumers are left with the choice of whether to use or not, and the price at this time becomes the maximum the consumers are capable of paying.

For instance, as customers using Google search engine are an absolute majority, advertisement companies have no choice but to pay the set price. In the same way, as Microsoft Windows OS and state infrastructures such as LPG and highways have no other choices due to their unique characteristics, suppliers' power is absolute. In particular, if services such as telecommunications and energy are monopolized in the countries with low level of domestic demand, consumers are disadvantaged. Conversely, the ultimate goal of companies is to have a monopoly in any way possible.

The customer contact platform principle came out as it became difficult for companies to have short-term profits as market competition increased, which is a survival principle that applies the monopoly.

Further Study: A Human Has 1,000 Faces

Carl Gustav Jung, a psychologist, stated, "Humans have thousand personas, and they make relationships wearing an appropriate persona according to situation." In other words, human beings change how they look depending on the other party in interpersonal relationships (whether intentional or not). Whoever one meets, the person changes his or her appearance depending on the others in a relationship, and the other parties interpret and define the person as they want. All human relationships operate this way. That is, the relationship between a person and others are not "one to N" but "N to N."

Era of N to N Platform

It is nearly impossible to realize the reality of N to N human relations in an online environment. A prime example is a post on a Facebook page which is exposed to everyone the person has made friends with. Therefore, only the plain content "harmless to anyone who reads" or implied expressions become posted. Or, at best, users create a group and wears a mask for each group.

More recently, Facebook users are steadily decreasing among teen users of SNS in the United States, and the proportion of those who stated that they trust Facebook is also very low, below 10 percent of the population. Adolescents who are not accustomed to wearing masks leave SNSs as easily as they jumped onto SNSs. The fundamental reason for decreasing teen users of Facebook or Twitter reveals their limitations are because they failed to express countless personas of human.

On the other hand, individual or group mobile messaging services, the platform based on diversity, are growing significantly. The "N to N platforms" represented by WhatsApp and WeChat allows emotional communication depending on social relationships with the other party instead of uniform expression of personal orientation.

For example, the current mobile SNS is not a simple communication service. Although it is currently focusing on expanding the customer contact platform, and it is its ultimate goal that users establish a complete social relationship network online as well as offline by conveying emotions as richly as in offline.

These show that many companies are making moves promptly in expanding, developing, and providing services such as messages, emoticons, backgrounds, gifts, photos, finance, and retail, which helps users express identity in their N to N relationships.

N to N Business

The concept of N to N platform is also found in the retail industry. Human beings are willing to invest time and money in the areas of their interest, but in other areas, they try to just follow others. In general, career women interested in fashion are indifferent to computer software or furniture assembly, and middle-aged men interested in electronic devices show no interest in trendy fashion or movies, and these orientations reflect consumption patterns exactly. After all, human and products and services are also in N to N relationships.

For instance, young women with a child compare women's clothes they are interested in meticulously in department stores or road shops and buy latest trendy products, while they buy their husbands' or children's clothes from affordable brands in the outlets. In addition, affordable shopping customers usually order low-cost food online, but for holiday gifts, they go to stores and buy the highest quality fruits.

The omni-channel strategy and 360 degree customer analytics, recent hot issues, also result from the need for this N to N platform. In the past, all marketing was concentrated on economically capable VIP customers, which is a very inefficient approach from a customer's point of view. In the present day of increasing diversity, only the companies which conduct optimal marketing of individual products and services using comprehensive customer analytics based on data for specific service channels are surviving.

PART 3
Data Is Created by Me

CHAPTER 7

Knowing Necessary Data Is Everything in Data Analytics

Necessary Human DNA Is Only 2 Percent

The Human Genome Project is the project to analyze all nucleotide sequences of chromosomes that determine human genes, which scientists in six countries, including the US and Japan, began in 1990 and finished in 2003. As a result, three billion pairs of DNA nucleotide sequence data, a human genetic blueprint, was cataloged with an accuracy of 99.99 percent. That is, humans have been converted to data.

Many scientists declared that this was an "important gift to humanity" and "application of this information will be a breakthrough for biology, medicine, and the society." They thought that as the analysis of human genome shows how genes are arranged, the causes of gene-related diseases, such as cancer and Alzheimer's in particular, could be precisely determined. People were filled with hope that finally the mystery of humans would be revealed and we would come close to God's realm of curing all diseases and re-creating organs.

However, this plan encountered an obstacle. They knew nothing about how to use DNA data. Genetic information contained in DNA is used for making proteins by mRNA. The activity of mRNA, a medium to transfer genetic information, is the key process of life processes, and analyzing the process is the key to solving physiological phenomena and diseases. Simply knowing nucleotide sequences does not allow understanding life processes and thus is useless by itself.

In addition, among the three billion pairs of DNA nucleotide sequences, only 2 percent serve as DNA. The remaining 98 percent lost their function as they degenerated in the evolution process. In other words, a life form processes and uses an extremely small particular portion of the enormous database called DNA. In conclusion, determining which DNA to use in what way emerged as the key to the success of the Human Genome Project. The biology community, where everyone believes that everything is likely to be solved with DNA sequence analysis, suffered a setback again.

Scientists could not identify trait expressing genes by simply analyzing DNA strands individually. This is because multiple DNA strands work together to create a single protein. It was necessary to find the secret of the process of combination of trait expressing genes in the entire DNA. This requires observing the phenomenon of actual genes being expressed, understanding the process in which the genes are created, and analyzing the principle.

Therefore, DNA analysis nowadays focuses on activity and needs of a life form. It starts from the fundamental question, "Which protein does a life form require in which condition?" For instance, using the results of genetic diseases or difference in physical structure, DNA analysis traces the development back to DNA patterns, and analyzes how DNA strands are combined to generate proteins.

The most important point is to observe and understand the essential needs of a life form and associated activities. DNA sequence data is unnecessary for this. The best approach is to forget about data, establish hypothesis from a perspective of life, and collect and process data.

Don't Boil the Ocean

The same logic for DNA analysis applies to data analytics. The amount of big data that the human race is currently retaining is as enormous as that of the DNA sequences. In this day and age, all substances and behavior data of human beings are recorded as data. Production data for 3D printing is growing, and music and paintings have also been converted into data. Thanks to ubiquitous computing technology, activity data is accumulating, including transaction data, location tracking, and CCTV footage.

Many companies try to integrate large data and build systems for use without clear plans, but this is the same as "boiling the ocean." To prevent this, we must learn lessons from past experiences, especially that of the software crisis. Compared to the rapid advances in computer hardware capacity and complexity, software development did not advance much. Hardware performs better and increases in value as development advances; however, software does not. This is because unlike system performance, applications must be developed "in the direction toward creating the value" in the use aspect.

As the diversity of participation in DNA database utilization has become possible and development potential has become unlimited since the Human Genome Project, big data also allows unlimited utilization and has growth potential. It is becoming a trend that big data from institutions such as public agencies is released to the public and its use promoted. Lately, it has become possible to obtain rapidly increasing social activity data using crawling (one of techniques to collect data from web). In other words, it is becoming easy to access a large amount of data even if the user is not a large corporation.

However, just as knowing three billion nucleotide sequences only cannot explain all life phenomena, big data alone can neither explain customer orientation nor lead to outcomes. How effectively can data be completely utilized is up to the person who tackles the problem. Present day data analytics is more about quality than quantity. Companies must identify needs and set goals from the customer's point of view, and create high quality data through collecting and processing necessary information. Contemporary global IT companies such as Facebook, Google, Amazon, and Apple strive to make their products and service intuitive and simple for human use. They process data to make it possible for users to use their services as easily as possible rather than making services complex and diverse for the same function.

Human and chimpanzees share as much as 98.7 percent of their DNA. This completely overturns scientists' prediction that the DNA of human beings as superior being would show significant differences from other animals. What is the reason for such a large difference between humans and chimpanzees despite nearly identical DNAs? This is because of the difference in expression of the same DNA; that is, an individual's characteristics are determined by how DNA is used. Human beings evolved by expressing traits necessary for high-level mental ability. As a result, they were able to win the competition against other animals, and the ability to utilize the DNA information acquired in the process became the core competency of humans.

In the future, core competency of humanity will be the ability to select, process, and use only the necessary information from large data. Therefore, it is the challenge of the future to create value by finding data that fits the purpose and to, then, process it appropriately, just like with DNA.

Smartwatch: To Whom to Sell?

Seeking the Impossible

A global IT company in the United States requested to build a data-based marketing strategy for wearable products. In particular, they asked for market research and a marketing strategy for smartwatches, which they prioritized through the enterprise.

The company's coordinator provided me with the company's customer data and asked me to analyze the purchase and transaction data. My response was simple: "Company data is not necessary at all." The coordinator looked puzzled at my response. They have accumulated a considerable amount of customer data and had a well-established product database. They have always used them for identifying customer characteristics and making marketing plans. Therefore, they expected that research for the new product, the smartwatch, would proceed in the same way.

When creating a marketing strategy, products and customers must be understood first followed by defining target customers. In the current smartwatch market, only a handful of early adopters exist. Moreover, among the customers of the company's products, nearly no early adopters who'd accept smart technology existed.

If it was for creating a marketing strategy for computer equipment or electric appliances, existing customer and product data would have been sufficient for analysis. However, creating a marketing strategy based on analysis of existing database in the context of no data on potential customers of smartwatches, a new market, is seeking the impossible.

Example of Potential Customer Classification for US Smartwatch Market

Characteristics		SNS sensitive	Self-managing women		Employed men	
Classification		Young women on SNS	Older self-managing women	Convenience-seeking & self-managing with higher education	E-mail, music, convenience-seeking economically capable men	Men indifferent to social activity & work technology
# of respondents		78	70	109	75	92
Preferred feature (for profiling & clustering, ranking survey & 7-pt scale standardization)	Control device	6.0	4.4	5.6	3.8	6.2
	Social media	3.0	6.4	6.4	6.4	3.9
	E-mail	2.4	4.3	4.4	3.5	2.5
	Stand-alone	6.9	6.1	2.8	3.3	2.4
	Music	3.2	5.2	4.1	3.0	5.2
	Healthcare	4.9	2.4	2.6	6.0	5.7
	Air & environment	4.4	3.7	3.4	6.3	6.4
	Voice recognition	5.3	3.4	6.6	4.4	3.8
Demographics (reference, relative 5-pt scale)	Proportion of men	43%	41%	47%	59%	58%
	Age	3.8	3.8	3.5	3.9	3.8
	Economic ability	2.4	2.6	2.4	3.4	2.8
	Education	2.2	2.1	2.7	2.3	2.7
Classification from technology adaptation perspective		2.7	2.6	2.6	2.5	2.7
		Browser	Trendy & mass appeal	Trendy & mass appeal	Innovator & early adopter	Conservative & mass appeal

* Must collect information on the targeted customer type

Therefore, the first thing that I did was to investigate the customer composition of the current electronics market and its characteristics. To achieve this, it was important to identify the positions of customers in terms of product adoption lifecycle. This is because the number of customers who accept and purchase new products is fixed, and the rest of the customers, the general public, purchase following these early adopters. I had to identify positions based on product adoption lifecycle by classifying all customers into categories and concentrate on the early customer group as the target customers for the smartwatch. This required customer data for the entire market, which had to be obtained separately.

I acquired data by conducting customer survey on customers' lifestyles and device use behavior, while understanding hidden needs by collecting relevant social big data. In addition, I selected highly reliable data, standardized the data, and conducted k-means clustering.

Customer surveys easily generate bias toward extreme responses, and it is easy for respondents to report differently from their true intentions. Therefore, items must be ranked in such a way so as to prevent customers from providing false responses, and the results must be standardized for interpretation.

The most suitable five clusters were selected as potential customers. This is just for classification for direction of marketing, not for personalized marketing. The clusters generated from clustering were interpreted using demographic information and smart device ownership information.

The results showed that the primary target cluster was the cluster of "e-mail, music, convenience-seeking economically capable men." They were found to be early adopters who adopt technology first and actively purchase new products. They required new technology for hobbies or to use for work rather than features such as SNS, healthcare, or voice recognition. They were above all craving for a stand-alone type with features that could be linked to various devices. They wanted email and music more.

Principles for Understanding Customer Clustering

As of 2015, the smartwatch product market is in the introduction stage. Therefore, the general public does not respond to smartwatch at all, and only early adopters are using them sporadically. If so, what are the criteria for identifying smartwatch early adopters among countless customers? To identify them, characteristics of early adopters must be defined using customer segmentation. Early adopters differ depending on products; therefore, positions of product adoption lifecycle must be defined from the perspective of customers who use specific products.

Let us take an example. Would fashionista customers in their 20s who enjoy Facebook and Instagram be early adopters? The answer can be both yes and no. Those who adopt fashion and SNS fast can be early adopters of fashion and SNS, but they are classified as general public in the case of smartwatch. This is because they consider their economic ability, and will not use smartwatches till they are popular. Moreover, early adopters of smart TVs and smartwatches are not identical. Therefore, customer segmentation must always be designed and conducted appropriately for targeted product and market.

The survey results showed that early adopters of smartwatch were men who are sensitive to IT and are economically capable. This customer group places a significant value on exposure to latest technology earlier than others, and the price was not a big issue because to their economic ability.

The Purpose of Data Analysis Is to Understand Customer's Behavior Principles

The early adopter customer group of the smartwatch market was above average in social status, and the proportion of smartwatch experience was relatively high. Although it is commonly thought that early adopters of smartwatch would want novel and fun features such as SNS, voice recognition, heart rate checking, and air and environmental data, the analysis results were quite different. The early adopters, "economically capable employed men," primarily wanted the feature to control other electronic products through IOT device compatibility in addition to basic convenience features used for work, such as e-mail.

Why would they want only the IOT control feature in a smartwatch, even though a variety of features such as heart rate checking, air and environmental data provision, and voice recognition exist? The answer can be found in the success of iPhone in the past.

Apple used previously existing technologies such as mobile phone, PDA, MP3, and touchpad, and introduced no new cutting edge features. It just made a smartphone by combining technologies which, then, the people could use easily.

It works the same for smartwatches. Since human perception does not change overnight, people do not require various high-technology features. To make a smartwatch, which is yet to grow, the company must choose one specific feature and make it easy to use to make it a hit. Smartwatch is the frontrunner of wearable devices. Therefore, the company must identify a hit feature that showcases the aspect of being always close to the user, the greatest advantage of wearables. Early adopters felt that the ability to control other devices was the most attractive aspect. This is because other features neither fully showcased the strength of being always close, nor were they features that they had sufficient previous experience with.

Ultimately for smartwatch, how much it can be linked to various devices through collaboration with partner companies using smart home/ IOT technology is the key to success. Hardware companies tend to configure products primarily with features they can develop easily, but this is not recommended. A single, emotionally based feature that customers require determines the choice.

Obtaining data does not mean the end of work. Rather, in big data analytics, the process of designing and interpreting data is more important. Designation of target customers, concentration on them, and identification of needs are priorities, which require convergent thinking that combines insight into humanities and statistical inference, instead of mere technological know-how. This is the ultimate direction of big data analytics.

Your Data is the Tip of an Iceberg

A data analytics team of a global retailer decided to calculate customer purchase cycles and provide the data to the marketing team. Analytics team tried to increase the purchase rate by calculating the cycle of customers purchasing products and conducting targeted marketing in accordance with the next purchase point in time. Initially, it sounds logical, because people purchase certain products periodically.

However, would it be possible for a retail company to predict it? Customers do not purchase products from one company only. For instance, if a customer uses one company whenever they buy shoes, the purchase cycle can be calculated accurately, but if the customers use multiple retailers to purchase them, the purchase cycle would not correspond to the actual cycle. Calculating it with the company's own data only leads to errors.

Catalina Marketing, a data analytics company, provides customized coupons by collecting data from various retail companies and calculating cycles. Having the entire purchase information like this, it can understand customers completely. Otherwise, one sees only one side of customers; therefore, it is difficult to know the purchase cycle pattern.

Customer Exit Prediction System

A global insurance company requested for my consultation while conducting customer segmentation using big data analytics. They requested consultation, stating they were conducting segmentation and customer value assessment using the company's own customer data, and they did not know how to segment customers due to insufficient data. In response, I introduced them to a case of a customer exit prediction system.

An insurance company developed a customer exit prediction system. It monitors behaviors of the customers of the insurance company and alerts the relevant insurance planner if there is a sign of exit. This was developed by selecting a few types of behaviors that are manifested before customers leave, based on statistical analysis of big data, and conducting ongoing monitoring. Having built the sophisticated quantitative system using data, the insurance company expected to have the effect of proactive response before customers leaving.

In a little while, an insurance planner heard of the system. In a few days, he received the list of customers who were predicted to withdraw, and the planner was shocked at the list. A customer on the list was none other than the son of the planner's best friend.

Wouldn't it be unlikely for the best friend's son to leave? Moreover, the planner knew it much better than the system. In fact, the insurance company implemented the system for a while, but no planners used the system due to the low accuracy of prediction. The system ended as a failure.

Finishing the story, I advised my client to stop their current customer analysis. The reason was because analyzing with insufficient data is useless. The organizations that analyze data usually try to generate results using their own database only. From the beginning, they consider external data irrelevant and exclude it. However, the primary task of data analytics is to understand customers accurately. If necessary, they must obtain necessary additional data using any means and strategies.

Database of insurance companies usually includes superficial data only such as agreement terms, period, demographics (region, age, gender, occupation, marital status), and renewal status. However, what would be the most useful information for understanding customers? It is the behavior process. Customers show many behaviors and undergo psychological changes as they get to know about an insurance product, make comparisons, and decide to purchase. This process is usually performed by insurance planners' sales. Although planners know customers' family information, social relationships, and even personality, they enter little of the information.

Internal data on insurance-related behavior shown once or twice a year can never describe a customer. It shows not the process but only the result of using insurance product. The attempt to determine customers based on the tip of the iceberg of result only is meaningless.

Therefore, I advised my client to collect external data by conducting surveys, interviews, and research, which specifies key points of the process of a customer selecting an insurance product. I advised them to cluster customers by collecting data on customer behavior process, and then, identify pain points for individual customer types by finding distinct characteristics that classify customer types.

How to Utilize Internal Data 200 Percent

This approach generates a doubt from the IT perspective. "Can this be viewed as a permanent data analytics implemented with a system?" The doubt is legitimate. The reason for us to conduct customer clustering using external data is ultimately to understand customers with internal data the company has.

The process is as follows.

1. Generate distinct characteristics of persona of each customer type based on external data.
2. Generate the method to determine individual types by classifying type-specific characteristics using internal data.

3. Process internal data (agreement information, demographic information, use information) based on the results of (2). For instance, to classify the customers of the "employed male sensitive to acquaintance sales" type among pension insurance customers, data such as "living in a small city," "low-to-middle economic ability," "having a young child," and "working in an established company" are processed and indexed.

4. Assign customers to clusters using the indexes generated in (3).

5. Understand customers using other internal data.

This approach enables understanding a significant part of customers just with a small amount of customer data and can be used in a wide range of applications such as sales, product sales, and needs prediction.

CHAPTER 8

Create Data

Picasso Is a Data Scientist

Picasso was one of the most creative and innovative artists of the 20th century. His finesse, originality, and humor were unparalleled; the domains of his work encompassed sculpture, printing, pottery, collage, and even poetry and plays.

Picasso is known as a cubist. However, what did the genre of cubism actually mean to Picasso? In fact, Picasso had no interest in cubism. He just wanted to express pure human thoughts and emotions. Cubism developed as a result of him expressing his philosophy without the confinement of means and methods; the genre was not very important to him.

Picasso focused on the diversity of people and associated principles from a relativistic perspective. Every human being has a unique perspective of the world, and own time and space. In particular, Picasso concentrated on painting the world seen from a child's eye.

His artwork includes a painting of a mother holding a child. The hands of the mother are more than twice as large as actual hands. In *Guernica*, humans and livestock are shown simultaneously. What do these figures express? From a child's perspective, a mother's hands feel huge as they provide care for and feed the infant. Citizens of a small city in Spain were similar to livestock—just means to an end—in the eyes of German soldiers.

Instead of painting the absolute landscape viewed the same by everyone, Picasso strived to express from the relativistic perspective. In the process of identifying many significant representative characteristics of a target and trying to paint them on a canvas, cubical forms emerged. If he tried to express them cubically from the beginning, the work we see now would never have been created.

However, many people misunderstand that Picasso became well-known by developing cubism. In following this way, many modern painters try to develop new concepts and unique art forms. However, this sequence is wrong. When an artist focuses on pursuing artistic purpose, the representation form becomes just a means. The framework of cubism interferes with creativity. Picasso concentrated on the problem (world seen from various points of view) and deliberated to find the solution regardless of means and methods.

The same goes with processing data. If the analyst focuses on the purpose and specifies the method logically, the strategy to utilize big data comes naturally.

Picasso was a competent data scientist. He extracted characteristics by analyzing data in a way that fits the purpose, created new results one by one by processing actual landscapes, and stored it appropriately in the database called a canvas. It does not matter what the actual landscape looked like. If one wants to see an actual landscape, one can take a picture of it with a high quality camera. Finding elements that can generate the value for humans and processing and using actual data from the perspective—this is the true sense of value creation and data analytics.

Data portraits customer feature

A global service business once inquired about methods of data analytics. I provided the following brief description on necessary data and processing methods: first, classifying customers into categories; second, indexing customer characteristics based on trade area, time of their use, billing amount, and frequency of use; and third, clustering customers. In addition, I also gave them a few example cases. Then, the person from the company asked me, "We also used data (e.g., trade area, time, amount, frequency) in the same way you do and have classified customers using the criteria, but we couldn't get the results we wanted. How do you process data to generate such a different result?"

I provided the answer using the story on Picasso's relativistic perspective. The same data looks different naturally if perspectives differ. If identifying hypothetical characteristics from customer's perspective, one can find the way to process data. It is just like food made with same ingredients that tastes completely different depending on the cook's skills.

If one looks at the data with a clear objective, appropriate data processing strategies come to mind. However, many companies take data processing to be a nuisance and run statistical software randomly by putting all large data and waiting for whatever that comes out. This ends up fruitless.

It is an unwise strategy to obtain averages and understand customers, relying solely on numbers such as time and amount when processing data. One must have a clear goal of segmenting and understanding customers according to marketing needs, based on the fundamental question, "Why do we want to understand customers?" One must first classify customers into hypothetical categories based on a general survey, and then define attributes to identify characteristics of each type before processing data.

For instance, if one wants to classify types of customers who use coffee shops for work among visitors of coffee shops, the following characteristics can be identified.

- Visiting during working hours (9 a.m. to 6 p.m. weekdays)
- Usually purchasing two to three items per visit
- Usually purchasing beverages
- High rate of purchasing the same product

If one attribute of proportion of visits during working hours is chosen among the characteristics, an index called "frequency of visits during working hours/total number of visits" is generated based on customer visit data. These indexes are put together for customer profiling, and this is used for clustering and marketing.

Re-creation of Human Networks of SNS Companies

It has always been very important to identify acquaintance networks because it makes possible to make sales through connections. However, in the offline era, only data from consultations and purchases could be obtained, and the rest of the activities were left for guesses or estimation. Therefore, there were limitations in understanding customer behavior. However, in the present day, a large amount of activity data is recorded online. From customer inflow pathways, to length of connection time, page views, information submitted, shopping cart, and movement of mouse cursor, the analysis of online data provides a significant amount of detailed information that can assist in understanding customer behavior, and this allows sophisticated modeling based on customer behavior.

Draw a Human Relationship Network Map

SNS companies retain algorithms on the "friend suggestion" feature. If so, what is the companies' friend finding mechanism? First, they define the purpose of suggesting a friend to customers. The primary purpose is not to simply increase the number of registered friends but to increase customers' SNS activities (i.e., their traffic) and turn them into loyal customers (e.g., using other content). Accordingly, relevant elements are ranked by scoring and weighing them, and suggesting a customer potential friends based on the ranks.

Suggesting acquaintances of customers' friends is the lowest level of suggestion. While conventional social services focused on surface information that customers submitted themselves, technologically advanced companies have focused on finding customers' acquaintances based on their behavior.

For instance, the question they always struggle with is, "What are the behaviors that indicate that people are in a social relationship?" To find this, first, companies brainstorm about customer behavior. Then, they define elements by finding traces of the behavior in the database, and suggest friends. The next step is to check if the customer's activity increases after accepting a friend by testing statistical significance.

Global SNS companies analyze friend potential using five types of information in general in order to trace hypothetical behaviors customers show when meeting a friend: (1) acquaintance relationship information, (2) information from external sources, (3) information on manifested interests, (4) personal activity information, and (5) location information.

First, acquaintance relationship information basically recommends the people in the groups the customer is affiliated with such as friends' acquaintances, fans, schools, and company. However, it is risky to suggest someone based on the fact that they share many friends. High school alumnus and the boss differ in the purpose and depth of relationship.

Therefore, such persons are identified who are most likely to be close to and ought to be closer using statistics, by combining all information including the nature of groups, the amount, frequency, and recency of conversation with people in the groups, and words used in the conversation. The goal is that the customer sends a friend request as a result of the friend suggestion, and later through relationship activities, SNS use increases.

Second, the information from external sources refers to the information on the friends outside the SNS. Relationships also take various forms, and the importance of a relationship depends on the form. To expand the platform in the beginning stage, SNS companies need to collect data from external sources by aggressively partnering with relevant companies, bringing external data, and making corporate acquisitions.

Third, companies use information on manifested interests. Customers are clustered based on their interests. The companies profile customers' interests by assembling information on behaviors such as enjoying movies, responding to economic newspapers, and viewing videos on sports, and suggest customers the people who are likely to be most similar to them.

Fourth, companies use information on personal activities such as photographic information. They trace acquaintances by tagging the people pictured together in photos uploaded on SNS, and adjust depth of relationship in accordance with frequency of being pictured together. In addition, they decide a suggestion type by calculating the closeness using text analysis of uploaded content.

Fifth, the use of location information is to suggest the customer group who shows similar reactions while a customer is posting on his or her location and activity, which suggests possibility of moving together, or suggest friends who engage in similar activities in nearby locations. Being more than a simple concept of location or place, area data sometimes locates optimal friends who show similar paths and behavior patterns as the customer's (using existing friend statistics).

Once these five types of data have been collected, customers must be clustered into types first. Suggestions can be made through network clustering or on an individual basis. A regression analysis is performed with individual attributes, in which data are standardized and designated as the input condition, and accepting friend request and activity index are designated as the output indexes. Then, friends with high probability of friend suggestions and activity can be identified among those in the suggestion list using regression coefficients of attributes in the analysis, and the companies suggest the friends continuously. Attributes and coefficients in the regression analysis constantly change due to personalization, and the model becomes more sophisticated as data accumulates.

Although friend suggestion is a simple feature, just using data cannot yield productive results. It must involve defining human social activity patterns hypothetically and creating an optimal model by finding behavioral patterns in data and indexing those behavioral patterns. This approach starts with human behavior. Once the strategy with a solid foundation is generated, data can be identified proactively, and processing the data to fit the purpose becomes easy.

Case Study

Are Buyers of Louis Vuitton Rich?

Louis Vuitton, which was sensational in the 2000s, successfully launched itself as a luxury brand. The brand became a big sensation, but the most sold products of the brand were reasonably-priced handbags. With luxury brands, different types of customers purchase products in different stages. Most women start with purchasing a reasonably-priced handbag. Customers with higher economic ability tend to move on to wallets and clothing in the listed order.

This is not limited to fashion and is found in all industries and products. Customers always begin purchasing with a basic product or promoted product (that everyone has due to its mass appeal and reasonable price) which generally has a lower barrier for entrance. They start with representative products of companies such as Apple's iPhone, Kiehls' moisturizing cream, and Converse's basic color sneakers. As they accumulate experience, they look for more unique and specific models in the second and third purchases.

This phenomenon can be considered as the process that reveals one's unique orientation. Orientations that were not shown in the early product purchase behavior (with little experience) are gradually revealed.

Companies may use this as a stage-specific loyalty building strategy. The process of building loyalty proceeds one stage at a time and does not skip stages. Customers do not take a gamble at the beginning. To the customer who has no Chanel product, pushing new Chanel products or special designs is ineffective. The company must suggest the most basic Chanel classic handbags and gradually create a portfolio. Customer management needs to take a stage approach. At the beginning, they must focus on trust building, and gradually move on to personalized response. The use of these customer experience stage principles expands customer purchases, and eventually, develops loyal customers.

Processing Customer Experience Stage Data: General Retailer

The use of data analytics customer segmentation techniques (profiling and clustering) discussed earlier reveals customers' unique orientations and characteristics. It must be noted, however, that customers of mature markets and growing markets must be treated differently. In the case of offline-based companies, which have customers with a great deal of experience and large accumulated data spanning a long period, customer segmentation results are interpreted as customers' unique orientations. However, in the cases of companies that are rapidly growing or with latest trendy products as in mobile retail, customers are often not very experienced. Therefore, customer segmentation results depend on the stage of customer experience and reveal characteristics accordingly.

A mobile platform retailer has implemented algorithms for loyalty building.

The results of customer clustering reveal clusters as shown in the figure, and reveal the orientations in the current state. Customer with more experience (i.e., customers with higher frequency of purchases and purchases of larger amounts) show more distinct characteristics. The results of verifying data according to the level of past experiences shows the pattern in which customers became more loyal as customer experience increased.

Customers begin to trust a shopping mall when they purchase products or services three times on an average and explore various aspects

Mobile customer experience stage cluster and loyalty building pattern

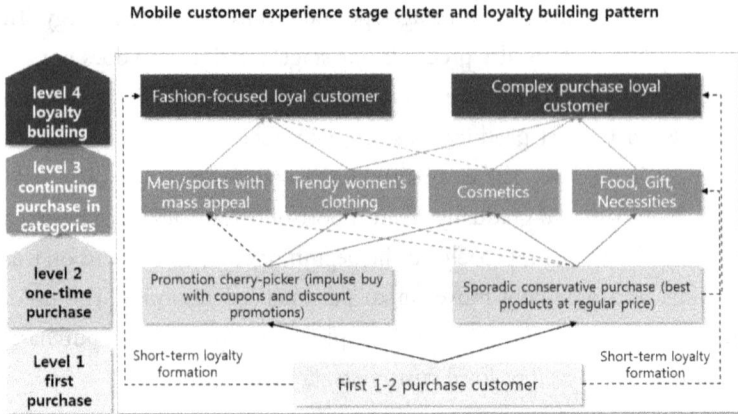

of the shopping mall 10 times that of purchasing on an average. After 10 times, they behave according to their own orientations, begin up-sell, and become VIP. In other words, customers become loyal in stages, and the loyalty building process for similar orientations shows specific patterns. Therefore, appropriate suggestions and purchase promotions were needed to be made by separating each stage of loyalty building.

Based on this model, we implemented algorithms to build customer loyalty and expand product sales. We cleared the barriers for customers in each stage and generated solutions to improve sales in each stage. Target marketing logic was created by increasing loyalty through suggestions for additional product purchase necessary to enter the higher stage. Using this logic and no additional cost, the company was able to increase VIP customers to twice as much as before.

Further Study: Shadowy Side of Data Processing

"Tomato on the Stem, and Potato on the Root"

In 2013, Thomson and Morgan, a UK horticulture company, achieved commercialization of "TomTato," which has tomatoes on the stem and potatoes on the root, and began selling them in countries including the UK and New Zealand. TomTato was developed by manually grafting stems of tomato and potato, allowing the harvesting of potatoes and cherry tomatoes from the same plant simultaneously. This achievement could have been a revolution in the agriculture industry and was expected to play a major role in solving global food crisis.

On the other hand, activists of Greenpeace, an international environmental organization, protest against genetically modified organisms (GMOs) on a regular basis. GMOs are crops that are made with DNA manipulation technologies. For instance, through DNA manipulation, new GMOs of high quality and resistance to pests and disease are mass produced.

Grafting and DNA manipulation share in common the phenomenon of creating high quality crops through plant processing. Then, why are people against DNA manipulation?

Don't Be Evil

Google made it a priority to meet consumers' search needs. Specifically, it focused on identifying and delivering "best information" through statistical algorithms and consumer intention analysis. As a result, it succeeded in securing a robust customer base and traffic; however, this did not translate into revenue. Therefore, it looked for a profit model, and the easiest to use was advertisements.

Many companies have difficulties in delivering product and service information to target customers. However, the use of Google's algorithms enables sophisticated selection of target customers, increasing the effect of the advertisement. Google first identified consumers' needs and provided search service; then, it identified businesses' needs and included advertisement in its target customers' search results. However, since search results and advertisements must be differentiated clearly, Google attached the label, "Google Ad" to prevent customers' misunderstanding. Moreover, it endeavored not to interfere with essential search features by keeping advertisements to no more than three lines.

Google's moto "Don't be evil" implies not to seek unjust profit through distortion of information while striving to provide consumers value. Distorting results for company's profits results in a loss of customer base and the platform in the end. To secure the platform from a corporate standpoint must have been a strategic choice; however, it is an exemplar that presented the way for IT companies founded on customers' trust.

Freemium

The problem all IT companies face is generating profits. No matter how hard a company strives to deliver value to customers and build brand recognition, if it fails to lead them to financial value, all its achievements can come to nothing. Therefore, companies must catch both: expanding the current platform and securing customers, and retaining driving force for future and growing through securing the profit model.

As a result, a profit model called freemium has been created. Freemium is a coined word of free and premium, indicating an approach of gradually generating revenues by monetizing advanced feature after attracting customers with free services. That is, it is to secure a cash cow while maintaining platform based on customer trust. Examples of the model include paid content on IPTV and Amazon's membership service and game items.

There is no correct answer regarding grafting and DNA manipulation. It is the same with data processing, and some have negative views. In capitalism, monetization is inevitable, and data processing is a great temptation to companies in that it encourages customers to pay consciously or unconsciously. Platform can disseminate incorrect information or make customers blind to outside world using data filtering. However, it must be reminded that data processing must proceed toward creating value based on customers' trust. From the moment a company distorts service through profit-based processing, consumers will turn away, and the company's value will fall in the long term.

PART 4

We Don't Need the Past

CHAPTER 9

Predict Human Unconsciousness

"I'm placing you under arrest for the 'future murder' that was to take place today at 8:04."

This is a scene from *Minority Report*, a Hollywood movie set in Washington, DC in the United States in 2054 that portrays the future of crime prediction. Stating this, the agents of the US Police Preventive Investigative Bureau arrest a husband who is watching the scene of his wife's affair for "future murder charge." The arrest is based on the prediction made by three Precogs that the husband would kill his wife and her lover. Placing the man who has not committed a crime under arrest without hesitation is possible because of the belief that the Precogs' prediction is correct "100 percent."

What is interesting about this movie is that it deals with future prediction. In the present day, business environment is increasingly uncertain, and predicting future is becoming harder and harder. Prediction is primarily used only for judging a company's value using analysis of companies, industries, and fluctuations in stock price; it is extremely rare to apply a model for predicting future with data to real life.

Would it be possible to predict future by analyzing past data? Since the beginning of this decade, predictive analytics has been growing rapidly. This is a separate field from consumer analytics, which analyzes consumers' behavior principles, which we have examined so far. According to a survey by Gartner Inc., this decade has seen companies' investment in predictive analytics software growing at an annual rate of around 10 percent.

Expensive Instrument Makes World-Class Musicians?

There are still many companies that expect that just running statistical analysis by putting data in with latest servers and software will automatically produce answers. However, if taking the approach of "Let's just run statistics, and it'll somehow give out an answer," most would fail. Even though one might succeed by luck, if the person does not know the principle of predictive analytics, he or she would experience limitation in use and would stop using it soon. That is, artists must be concerned about skills rather than expensive instruments. Instruments are good enough at the current level.

The most important thing in predictive analytics is intuitive design. The process starts with logical explanation of antecedent process (i.e., the cause). Box office predictions must start with the question, "Why would customers watch this movie?", customer complaint prediction must start with the question, "In what situation would someone complain?", and construction equipment predictions must start with the question, "Why do people construct?" The process of generating predictions varies across different types of antecedents. Just as different contractors have different reasons for buying construction equipment, applying a single standard (i.e., an attribute) to all different types reduces accuracy of prediction. Therefore, the essence of predictive analytics process is classifying types of antecedents, predicting based on key attributes for each type, and adding up results.

Heinrich's Law

On July 24, 1915, the SS Eastland, a large US steamer for passenger tours was shipwrecked on the Chicago River and 844 passengers were killed or went missing. Did the accident occur with no warning signs? If the accident occurred randomly, it could not have been prevented because no human being without omnipotence can know the future. However, all accidents and events are bound to have antecedent attributes. If these antecedent attributes are analyzed, accidents can be prevented. Rather than concentrating just on prediction, it is more important to identify the causes. Furthermore, it is the ultimate goal of data analytics to address the cause in advance.

Herbert William Heinrich, who dealt with countless accident statistics, discovered the statistical law using industrial accident case analysis. Specifically, he found that if there was one serious injury from an industrial accident, there had been 29 minor injuries and 300 potential injuries that could have happened previously for the same cause. This 1:29:300 ratio is called Heinrich's Law.

What is the implication of this for big data predictive analytics? It is that accident occurs in a series of process that are causally linked. Individual causal factors of potential injuries and minor injuries in combination become a cause of serious injury later. Therefore, in big data predictive analytics, classifying causal factors into types and managing them can prevent accidents in advance.

Regarding the causes of the SS Eastland disaster, various reasons were mentioned including excessive cargo loading and structural extensions, poor response by maritime traffic control center, irresponsible crew, and government's inadequate response. Predicting such maritime accident using data analytics is done in the following order:

1. Clearly define and classify accident types (e.g., shipwreck, building collapse).
2. Collect actual cases of accident, including potential injuries, minor injuries, and serious injuries, based on Heinrich's Law.
3. Identify major causal paths of accidents (e.g., cargo overload, structural extensions, control center's response, crew's competency, government response).
4. Identify frequent causal factors that are common across accidents; however, the factor needs to be inferred from behaviors of those involved. (For instance, if we look for a causal factor for excessive cargo load, relevant data could be relatively high transportation sales, records of discipline for those involved, and customer complaint data—be mindful of feasibility of data collection)
5. Convert these factors into numeric, standardized, and dummy variables, and perform regression analysis on them with the variable on accident status. Use them in a unit of specific period, repeating with modified weights of individual factors in order to increase sophistication of accident prediction.

These cause-based predictive analytics can be used in the following areas: (1) growth item prediction, which predicts hit products, brands, and industries; (2) demand prediction of stock and order-based industry market event sensing (i.e., indexing); and (3) risk and crime prediction in financial industry such as banks, insurance companies, and credit card companies, and public corporation such as tax offices and the police.

Now, let us take a look at specific applications for individual cases.

Big Data Predicting Human Unconsciousness

A global financial corporation requested me to provide consultation regarding the introduction of a risk detection and prediction system based on employee behavior. They wanted to detect employee-driven risks in advance by analyzing employee orientation and risk scenarios for special situations. As corporate crimes have increased recently, including leaked confidential information, embezzlement, aiding fraud, and leaked customer information, the company was deliberating the measures to take for risk behavior prediction for officers and employees of the company. They already had basic strategies in place. They had decided to select attributes using internal data and run statistics based on the time factor and were struggling to determine the servers and software to use.

However, I advised them that running statistical software without a plan for application is likely to fail. It is very dangerous to have a vague attitude that "once data is analyzed, prediction method will emerge" without a clear hypothesis or logical plan. Therefore, to introduce the risk detection system, I designed a prediction application based on the behavior principle of officers' and employees' perspective as follows.

1. Classifying risk behavior
   Classify risk behaviors into types. Risks are categorized based on previous experiences of large losses, such as employee leaking customer

Predictive analytics that fails

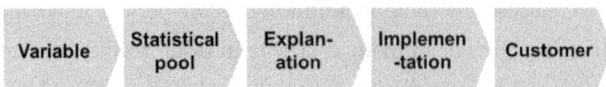

| Variable | Statistical pool | Explan-ation | Implemen-tation | Customer |

information and taking major secrets of the company. These are risks to detect from the point forward. For each risk, the level that employee's characteristic or unusual behavior is clearly differentiated is established as the classification criterion.

2. Defining and classifying the types of risk personnel
Generate a definition of hypothetical personnel for each risk type. For instance, those who leak company secrets or customer information include "the type that steals large data at other's request," "the type that takes out only the key information for specific purpose," "the type that steals information first, and later leaks it for personal use or a deal," and "the type that steals information for personal interest or backup." Different types show large variation in backgrounds including position, department, gender, marital status, parenthood, average time spent working outside office hours, salary, etc. Thus, the circumstances of engaging in risk behavior can be inferred based on these background factors.

3. Collecting actual cases of risk behavior and personnel
Collect actual cases of risk behaviors prior to analyzing data. An important reminder in this process is that as Heinrich's Law suggests, the number of potential risk behaviors is much higher than the number of actually revealed risk behaviors. If the actual cases of risk behaviors are insufficient, it is impossible to obtain statistically reliable results. Therefore, the personnel in charge in each department need to identify risk behaviors with maximum precision and collect all the cases. In addition, the information on the employees involved (e.g., demographics, administrative statistics) are also to be collected.

4. Processing and generating data attributes for prediction of risk behavior and personnel
Generate data attributes of individual cases of risk behavior. Usually, data from the previous six months is analyzed. Key attributes vary across risk behaviors. Key attributes include search keywords with search engine, checking out company regulations, frequency and time of archive room visits, details of working outside office, frequency and time of computer printout, details of e-mails sent outside, details of messenger use, etc. These are the data required for behavioral analysis, and in the event the data is not in place, a plan

to collect the data is established to use in improving the prediction model later.

5. Classifying risk personnel type

   Classify risk personnel types based on risk behaviors. Types are classified by performing profiling and clustering on all staff of the company using key data attributes.

6. Establishing weights of individual attributes using dummy regression analysis

   An essential process of predictive analytics with data is standardization and dummy coding. Data attributes such as frequency, time, proportion, amount, and status of use vary in characteristics, and some of them are difficult to quantify. Performing linear regression analysis with the nonlinear attributes results in bias. Therefore, data must be prepared for regression analysis by standardizing (e.g., ranking, natural log of the amount) the data that can be standardized; otherwise, data must be dummy coded.

   For instance, salary and risk do not increase at the same rate. Thus, the natural log of salary is taken to compare salary with the risk level, or dummy coded by dividing salary into intervals that are assigned 1 or 0. In dummy coding, it is important to divide data into intervals appropriately, considering the number of cases in each interval. If there are too many intervals, parameters for each interval decrease, increasing statistical errors, and if there are too few intervals, variation within an interval is ignored, leading to inaccurate prediction.

   A regression analysis is performed by selecting independent attributes that have the lowest level of association with other attributes, and setting the Y variable as the status of risk behavior (1 or 0). The coefficients of individual attributes within the margin of error, according to the results of regression analysis, are weights of the attributes; the sum of attributes multiplied by respective coefficients are obtained on a weekly basis by keeping the coefficient constant and inserting attribute data. This value is the risk probability.

7. Calculating individual probability of risk behavior by running automated applications weekly

   Calculate risk probability by running risk prediction software (for each risk type) weekly on the entire staff. Identify the cases with a risk probability above a certain level every week, and determine the cause by showing attributes' values as detailed reasons. If necessary, closely examine the personnel and the circumstances to prevent risk behavior.

8. Testing the model using back-testing for a specific period
Update individual weights using quarterly regression analysis. In addition, find additional data attributes and include it in regression analysis. Nowadays, a lot of attributes that fit specific purposes can be obtained using log data. As the amount of data, types of cases, and discovered risk behaviors increase, the system becomes a constantly evolving big data application with an increasingly sophisticated model.

The behavior principle predictive model of this case differs most from regular predictive models in that its focus is on principle of human behavior. Most companies ask, "Why do you categorize personnel into types, since we can run statistical software using data including web search logs, records on entrance and exit, printer use, history of accessing files and data, and e-mails for the entire staff?" I have also tried the strategy myself, but in most cases, I could not use the results because error rates were too high.

In predictive analytics, it is most important to classify types of different personalities and behaviors based on human judgment as much as possible. To do that, inferences on behaviors are made hypothetically from a human (or a customer) perspective, and then, regression analysis or prediction software for each type is used, borrowing the power of statistics. This is the most accurate strategy for predictive analytics that we can employ.

Another reason for focusing on behavior principle is because fundamental solutions can be found only when the principle is found. Once the principle is found, prevention and fundamental treatment

Principle of predictive analytics

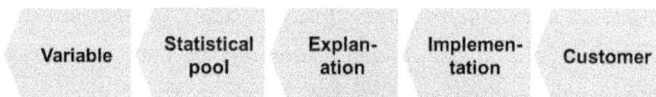

| Variable | Statistical pool | Explan- ation | Implemen- tation | Customer |

are possible. For instance, since the probability of risk behavior varies across personnel types, the personnel with high probability who require special attention can be effectively managed through personnel decisions. Moreover, company policies can be reorganized, and security can be enhanced for the paths of movement for specific types of personnel.

The reason why many people find the principle-based predictive analytics approach difficult is that it requires competencies in both humanities and engineering. Inferring human behavior principles and identifying attributes require knowledge in humanities, while programming using a statistical model requires engineering competencies.

Financial Risk Prediction

In online shopping malls, convenient payment is the essential component for customer retention. Then, how can companies catch both rabbits—keeping it both convenient and secure?

Global online shopping malls such as eBay and Amazon configure and manage security modules by applying the concept of risk prediction model examined earlier. This model, called the fraud detection system (FDS), first analyzes users' behavioral patterns. They define behavior patterns by recording users' purchase details and analyzing the data. Behavior patterns are identified as much as possible from the data recorded at the time of the purchase. This includes the categories of products, the quantity of products, the device used to purchase, and the region from where a user frequently purchases.

For frequent purchases, users can make a payment without a complicated authentication process. However, in the event that a payment transaction deviates significantly from the observed pattern, the payment system employs additional checks.

The system identifies the behavior pattern that causes fraudulent activity from a financial criminal's standpoint. That is, it classifies types of process used in committing crimes based on a financial criminal's behavior principles. Specifically, after identifying data attributes based on analysis of previous cases of risk behavior, the system calculates probabilities of a similar pattern being observed and sends out alert signals accordingly. In this situation, identification procedure is enhanced using the additional authentication as a warning to the customer and potential criminal.

The algorithms based on human behavior principles can be used in diverse cases and in a clear fashion. Both risk detection and sales forecast are based on human behavior. Unless starting from human behavior principles or psychological factors, sophisticated data analytics cannot be performed, and analytics ends up being superficial.

Professor Gerald Zaltman at Harvard University stated that only about 5 percent of our thinking occurs in the conscious mind. This is a testament to the importance of identifying essential needs and behavior principles of the human unconscious. In data analytics, the one who searches the deepest part of human behavior principles becomes the ultimate winner.

Case Study 1
Big Data Crime Prevention System

A Chinese big data company asked me to provide consultation on a criminal detection system. They were looking for ways to identify criminals effectively. Introducing them to the case of National Crime Agency in the UK, I proposed a model based on criminal behavior principles to them. Conventional data crime investigation approach is based on mathematical models, and it identifies patterns and predicts the future statistically by using attributes such as region, weather, and sporting events. At that time, there was no approach based on human behavior principle.

Although arrest rates had increased, crimes had not decreased. This was due to just trying to suppress crimes with police power without addressing social ills. In other words, the crime-predicting power might have been good, but preventing crimes at the fundamental level was impossible.

Durham regional police collected information on suspicious insurance claims from some large insurance data. The police ran hypothetical insurance fraud simulation on the data with actual people and their circumstances at the time. Discovering many characteristics of each type, the police monitored characteristic indicators. As a result, they were able to predict with high level of accuracy the organized insurance scammers who operated insurance scams.

Furthermore, the police investigated the larger question of the reasons for insurance fraud. Behind insurance frauds, various reasons existed including economic difficulty due to reduced income, information obtained by experience of receiving insurance money, and urgent need for a large sum of money, and the causes could be classified into types. Examination of indicators such as family, friends, changes in income, and history of contacting insurance company can reveal the reason for planning an insurance fraud. Police identified the underlying cause of each type, responded promptly, and implemented correctional programs. Moreover, for the cases that could not be resolved with police data or law enforcement only, government agencies collaborated to resolve the problems with a comprehensive investigation.

As shown above, principle-based predictions have high accuracy and applicability. The big data analytics modeling process that focuses on principle-based crime prevention is as follows.

1. Classification of crime types
   First, classify types of crimes that require prediction. Define them at the level at which cause and consequence of crime can be clearly differentiated (e.g., theft, violence, sexual crime, fraud).
2. Identification of types and behavior analysis of hypothetical criminals
   When generating types of criminals, focus on identifying characteristics of criminal that reveal the cause of a crime (e.g., economic, violence, sense of inferiority, depressive disposition).
   For each type of criminal, investigate cause of behavior using interviews and case analysis, and conduct simulation on pathways to crimes.
3. Identification of key attributes that indicate characteristics of criminals
   Find as many attributes as possible that can clearly reveal the type of criminal. Then, develop the logic to identify the attributes from databases. For instance, the probability of poverty-driven theft is high when the education levels are lower than high school, over a 12-month period of unemployment, and less than six months from

time of release from prison. Use the attributes by processing the attributes to reveal the type of hypothetical criminal. For instance, if the education level attribute must be included, rather than using a number, such as education years from 1 to 20, divide it into less than college education and college education or higher to make the hypothetical criminal type clearly understood.

Commonly used data are as follows:

- Statistical attributes: gender, age, economic ability, residence, education level, history of disease, family relations, etc.
- Crime attributes: number and length of incarcerations, date of release from prison, etc.
- Individual attributes: loss of job, reduction in asset, length of unemployment, childbirth, divorce, separation, etc.

4. Criminal profiling and clustering

Summarize attributes of criminals of each type of crime. Then, generate clusters of criminals for each crime type by performing statistical clustering. For instance, for the theft type of crime, categorize criminals into clusters such as reduced income cluster, mentally unstable cluster, and socially discontent cluster.

5. Estimation of crime probability

Estimate crime probabilities based on time, region, and individual using regression analysis by designating regional characteristics (e.g., education level, economic ability, population density, commercial districts, police force range), external factors (e.g., people's movement paths, weather, season, status of special event, weekend, time), and clusters and key attributes of criminals, as X variables, and crime outcome data as the Y variable. However, use attributes by dummy coding or standardizing them as necessary.

6. Crime prediction based on time, region, and individual

Predict risks of individual crime types, size of crime, and crime probability for individual time zones, and regions where an event (e.g., special event, holiday, and sports game) is held. Using the estimated probabilities and sizes, enhance security and optimize allocations of police force. Estimate crime probability for each individual, based on the cause index of each crime type, and monitor the individual's regular routes and unusual behaviors.

7. Crime prevention

Investigate root causes of individual crime types and identify solutions for them. For instance, investigate if a particular crime type requires job programs, medical support, or financial consultation. Seek cooperation from relevant agencies for each type, discuss solutions for each individual, and run a campaign if necessary. Identify social and economic problems and make them issues for collaboration among agencies.

Case Study 2
Predict Leaving Customers with Big Data

A luxury department store in the United States decided to use big data to predict and manage VIP customers' leaving. The data analytics team built a system that detected and predicted customer leaving using statistical techniques.

However, this system had two significant weaknesses. First, it was able to predict only the customers who clearly left. This system used the approach of detecting customer's leaving after identifying characteristics using the results of customers who left. Therefore, it generated obvious results like customers who have not visited for a long time or could not be contacted after repeated attempts were leaving customers. This was simply a confirmation of the fact that the sales team already knew. The system that predicts the results that anyone can figure out is not particularly helpful.

Second, the company could not take actions because it did not know why customers left. The data analytics team set the turnover as the target, instead of cause of turnover, and indicated the risk of turnover using simple indicators such as high, medium, and low. They analyzed no other characteristics.

The ultimate goal of the department store in using the process was not simply predicting customers' turnover but turning the customers who will leave to become loyal customers. How can a company win customers back without knowing why they leave? The company must first determine if the identified customers could be won back or not, and if they could be won back, analyze what problems made them leave.

When a customer leaves, there is a reason. The customer may switch to a competitor or move. If the customer switches to a competitor, there is a more specific reason (e.g., price, service, sales strategy, quality). The attitude of the data analytics team—predicting customer leaving only, without even asking a reason—is not short of the attitude of convenience-seeking detached indifference.

In relation to this aspect, I advised them to focus on identifying causes instead of trying to predict customer turnover. This is similar to the prediction based on causes of crimes discussed earlier. If focusing on why a customer leaves, it becomes easy to predict the turnover and win them back. This is because the ultimate goal is not to predict the turnover but to prevent the turnover in advance.

1. Identifying types based on the cause of turnover
    Based on customer surveys, observations, and interviews, identify the key reasons for customer turnover. Identify types and related representative characteristics of each type.
2. Defining the criteria of turnover
    Clarify the turnover criteria of each type. Indicate the degree of leaving numerically by specifying the periods (e.g., no visit for six months). Determine the time taken by the company to respond; it is defined differently across different types of turnover.
3. Establishing the win-back strategy for individual turnover reasons
    Prior to predicting turnover, determine if the customers can be turned around. If a customer has moved or has reduced economic ability, he or she cannot be won back no matter how much the company may try. The win-back strategy is also necessary to assess the importance of the customer who left in each type.
4. Establishing the database building strategy for individual types
    Each type has unique warning signs of turnover in data. For instance, middle-aged women fashion customers tend to reduce purchasing their own clothing before turnover. This is because they are picky about buying their own clothing, while they pay less attention to purchasing their spouse' and children's clothing, and once they buy their clothes in other department stores, they end up leaving as they buy all clothing in other department stores. Based on these

leading indicators, turnover types are classified and customers are assigned.

5. Regression analysis on customer turnovers

   Estimate coefficients and turnover probability for individual customers, using dummy regression analysis for each type by designating the status of turn over as the Y variable, and data characteristics (leading indicators) as the X variables.

6. Actions for individual turnover reason

   Identify customers with high turnover probabilities on a regular basis and take actions appropriate for the reasons (e.g., sales strategy, promotion, information provision). In addition, establish enterprise-wide response solutions by identifying the cause of turnover.

Further Study: Is Big Data Big Brother?

Big Brother is a fictional character in *1984*, George Orwell's novel, a mysterious dictator of a totalitarian state, Oceania. Big Brother monitors and controls citizens through telescreens. Citizens constantly feel that they live in a controlled society, under surveillance and suspicion rather than feeling protected.

Entering the era of big data, concerns are growing over leak of personal information and government surveillance. Although the concerns are clearly legitimate, regarding the use of big data, a more rational and logical approach is required. Will big data actually become the evil oppressive control for us?

The philosophy of big data use can be found in psychotherapy. Psychotherapy starts by identifying the underlying cause of patient's expression of emotions rooted in developmental stages. Provision of treatment comes later. In the same way, data analytics also identifies root causes by focusing on human behavior principles rather than the surface phenomena. The goal is to solve the problem.

The ultimate goal of data analytics is to enrich human lives. It does not conform to the so-called Big Brother's goal of surveilling and controlling people. The central idea of big data is perpetual creation of value by identifying and addressing the causes of human behaviors.

For instance, crimes are committed for a reason, and if the cause is not identified, ultimate solution is difficult to find. Surveillance and control is the worst way of using big data. In fact, strictly speaking, Big Brother and big data are clearly separate. Surveillance at the surface is Big Brother, and identifying internal principles and solving problems are big data.

Punishment or Prevention?

An official in criminal justice that I met said the following: "Catching criminals well does not mean that crimes decrease." What does this mean? It means that catching and locking up criminals at the surface level without solving the underlying cause of crime leads to other problems (e.g., new crimes, lack of policing, lower quality of life). This is the so-called balloon effect, the term to sound an alarm about the behavior of focusing on result only without addressing the cause.

Society does not advance by just predicting crimes precisely, as in the movie *Minority Report*. We must focus on addressing the cause of crimes. This corresponds to the direction of big data predictive analytics for crime. By concentrating on the cause of crime, it predicts crimes and reduces crime rates.

CHAPTER 10

Anything with a Pattern Can Be Predicted

A well-known boxer introduced the principle of avoiding a punch in an interview:

"It is too late if you try to avoid a punch after seeing the punch. You have to avoid it before it is thrown by watching the timing and rhythm of the opponent's movement." In fact, the time to avoid a punch is just 0.16 seconds. It is impossible to avoid it after seeing it. Therefore, one must avoid it based on preceding data of a punch.

Boxers first accumulate opponents' data as they throw jabs. They gradually recognize opponents' patterns by analyzing data unconsciously. It is then that they are able to predict a punch and avoid it. It is the same with data analytics. Just as no boxer is without a pattern, no business phenomenon is without a pattern. If there is a pattern, anything can be predicted.

Since the beginning of the 2010s, the fashion industry has been experiencing a serious slump. The only companies that are growing are SPA companies such as Zara and H&M. The market is controlled by online and mobile B2C retailers such as Amazon and eBay. What led to this?

Traditionally, fashion experts have manufactured and sold clothing, using ideas from famous designer collections which follow seasonal changes—spring/summer and fall/winter. However, this process that requires several months has the problem of being a completely supplier-centered manufacturing process. As consumers' fashion needs are changing constantly and the trend cycle is becoming shorter, such an approach to manufacturing and sales on a seasonal basis, an approach effective in the past when supply was short, is no longer effective.

In contrast, SPA companies monitor consumer needs on an ongoing basis and produce and distribute popular items fast. This is a typical consumer-centered process. SPA's style of operating (i.e., the business type) is considered as the inevitable outcome of the business environment changing from a supplier-centered to a consumer-centered process.

Contemporary fashion companies focus on clearly defining targets and their needs (i.e., product trends). Then, what is the strategy for discovering customer needs for fashion products using data analytics? The strategy is to identify the pattern of fashion trends following the prediction principle mentioned earlier. Then, the process must be framed, and approached in stages. Now, let us take a look at the trendy product prediction approach based on my experience with the fashion industry project.

Prediction Method Using Company's Internal Data

The following is the trendy product prediction and response model for an online fashion shopping mall used in my project.

1. Conducted profiling and clustering by analyzing customers' purchase data that was in the company's database. Based on the results of the analysis, generated customer orientation clusters and analyzed the characteristics of the clusters using interviews and research.

2. Conceptualized the customer groups based on stages of their responses to trends. Fashion products always spread following the sequence of trend stages. Strong trends spread to all customer groups, and weak trends run their course after spreading only to some. Identified and defined early adopters of trends among customer groups by developing customer early index (i.e., those purchasing new product early), and sneezer index (i.e., those purchasing hit product faster than others).

3. After identifying items early adapters purchase first, statistically analyzed their sales by period in the subsequent periods, based on sales volume, sales speed, and repurchase rate of the items.

4. Assigned trend attributes to each product. The trend attribute is an antecedent index for trend and includes the mean age, the proportion of those living in a metropolitan area, the proportion of mobile shoppers, and the gender of purchaser.

5. Performed regression analysis by standardizing statistics of early adopters' responses and products' trend attributes. Generated a regression equation using the results.
6. Predicted sales volume and revenues for all products using the regression equation.
7. Once the error of estimated sales volume was within limits, placed order and managed inventory.
8. Picked two or three potential hit products and pushed them up as the company's leading products through intensive marketing. In other words, sold popular products to target customers earlier than competitors by analyzing sales patterns of the products early.

The online shopping mall that I worked on was able to dominate the trendy fashion market using this trendy product prediction model only.

Prediction Method Using External Big Data

A fashion brand editing shop implemented a trendy product lineup system. This system required external data on early adopter customers other than the company's customers, as the company had little usable customer data because it was primarily an offline company. Moreover, in the case of shoes as the key fashion item of the company, once purchases are made in the store, it is already too late to secure inventory or conduct marketing; therefore, it had to collect data for preemptive actions. This is what was done:

1. Used the customers who use SNS in order to monitor the movement of the early adopter customer group. Selected as many places early adopters usually hangout as possible by reviewing online communities and SNS groups.
2. Collected posts of the customer group using data crawling and detected the initiation of fashion trends by combining the words frequently used. Automated trendy product and brand sensing by analyzing all posts focusing on specific words and descriptors. As traffic and frequency increased, the margin of error decreased and signs of increasing needs of the items in the future emerged.
3. Employed a strategy for the entire store to be renewed with hottest trendy products on an ongoing basis by monitoring fashion items

while quickly stocking the products to keep in the store through negotiation with target trendy brands. As a result, the company became known as an essential destination for offline early adopters through word-of-mouth.

4. Automated product lineup and inventory stocking (weekly estimated sales volume, order volume, security stocks) in accordance with trend strength for individual product indicated by big data, and established the system in which predictive power improves as data accumulates by optimizing it to reduce error of inventory as the system was implemented.

How to Predict One Step Ahead of Your Competitors

Retailers and manufacturers working in the field know the principles of spreading fashion trends. Data analytics is to create an easy-to-use solution using statistical analysis that they are unable to perform, applying the principles in the field. This requires understanding customer behavior and the principle fashion spreads that field agents already know.

A fashion company with a nationwide business network built a trendy product tracking system based on the trend spreading paths. A fashion trend starts by innovators and early adopters in the place of cultural and material exchanges, usually a port city (except luxury goods, the trend of which begins from the wealthy areas of economically-able cities). The trend spreads to the center of the city along the paths fashion customers move and eventually reaches large cities. Once the trend spreads among large city customers, it spreads throughout the nation to the customers who have not been exposed to the trendy items.

Casual padded jumpers were initially popularized by juvenile delinquents in a port city who romanticized violence and this soon spread as a trend among students. Then, it spread to large cities, becoming a hit. Later it spread to small cities, and in the end, to older customers.

In the case of luxury goods, the pattern is slightly different, and luxury products are purchased initially in heavily populated places. It goes through a long introduction stage, followed by purchases primarily by local customers, then, a growing number of customers who desire for it respond, spreading to the areas with economic ability. Then, it draws major attention, and fake products show up, becoming a nationwide trend.

This was also found in the case of marketing of Mizuno, a sports product company, in Brazil. In 2011, running shoes called *Prophecy* priced at BRL 999 came out on the market. Considering the economic level in Brazil, it is almost as much as US$1000.

At the beginning of the sale, only a handful of customers with economic ability living in the capital Brasilia bought them. Then, Prophecy increasingly established itself as the symbol of wealth through word-of-mouth, and became desired by the public. Then, as the 30-month installment payment promotion drew enthusiastic reaction, the popularity of Prophecy spread to the next rich city, Sao Paolo, leading to nationwide boom in Brazil.

As mentioned earlier, data analytics must be preceded by understanding of customer behavior and trend spreading principles. Conducting data analytics with clear objectives along with understanding can lead to big gains with small efforts. Using the trend spreading principles, I provided consultation services for a fashion retailer which had stores throughout the country, and the process was as follows.

1. Determined the fashion trend spreading sequence of individual stores using past product sales data. Created an index for monthly trend spreading sequence and compared the stores on the index.
2. At the beginning of trend spreading, opened flagship stores in port cities and checked how much popularity trendy items were gaining and how the popularity was spreading by monitoring daily the stores that were ahead in the trend spreading sequence. Conducted trendy product sensing by conducting research on design and brand demands focusing on trendsetting and trend spreading areas.
3. Once an item that flags a major trend was identified, conducted an intensive marketing for nationwide trendsetting while securing inventory.
4. Linked all of these to the system in order to incorporate them into logistics and marketing management automatically. This led to the success in enhancing competitiveness including cost saving in inventory management, increasing sales volume, and trendy item-targeted marketing.

Case Study 1

Forecasting Stock Price Fluctuations

In early 2011, Derwent Capital in the UK made profits by selling Twitter analytics-based algorithms. It determined the investors' investment psychology by analyzing about 10 percent relevant tweets out of millions of tweets. While returns for regular hedge fund management stayed at 0.76 percent in July 2011 when S&P500 index dropped by 2.2 percent, Derwent recorded 1.86 percent returns, demonstrating its performance. It was an example of creating profits by combining basic data with unstructured SNS data.

As this suggests, it is increasingly common to raise return on investment through share price prediction using data analytics. kabu.com in Japan provides customers with data analytics service with share price prediction model, and in the case of the United States, it generates high ROI by developing share price prediction model that combines algorithm sales and twitter primarily for hedge funds. Smartphone investment apps that use big data are springing up everywhere.

Currently, over 75 percent of NYSE transactions are handled by robots. The financial investment market is undergoing a gradual yet gigantic shift from human-based investment to computer-based investment. In the future, the financial market will become a warzone for machines and algorithms instead of people.

In keeping with this enormous trend of algorithmic trading, top-rated programming languages such as YesTrader and CybosTrader are showing up on the market. Using these programs, a trading system can be created by setting trading rules, and technical aspects that can be implemented based on information are currently nearly unlimited. Various conditions can be programmed such as, "buy shares if it rains," or, "sell at the current price if the Chinese market falls by over 5 percent." Using these algorithms, transactions can be made in real time automatically.

Moreover, the model can be verified using market data from the past 10-year period. Algorithms that respond to data changes in the future through self-learning based on machine learning technique can also be implemented. As these suggest, all technical infrastructure for financial investment based on data analytics is in place. However, no matter how great infrastructure is, designing and making an investment plan is a job for humans.

Which Data is Important?

Winton, a London-based data analytics company, determines transaction time and price of coffee using data analytics. The company makes predictions using clear understanding of the types and scenarios that cause fluctuations in coffee price and using the related factors instead of simply using leading indicators of coffee price. It identifies factors associated with fluctuations in coffee price in the database using software. Specifically, it examines factors such as coffee yields, strengths and circumstances of the economy of coffee producing countries, currencies, and coffee demand. Using the information, it makes predictions of types of situations of fluctuations in coffee demand and supply. For individual types generated using the process, key factors that influence price for each type are identified, and the algorithms that predict price according to changes in the factors developed.

Each demand-supply scenario has small but important signs. It is important to make predictions one step ahead based on these signs. Not all data is of equal importance. Proper weights need to be established using the type-specific scenario plans.

Companies and industries can increase sales, make profits, and change share prices through a variety of scenarios. These scenarios include increasing demands, competitor's leaving, and political events occurring in a specific market. Each scenario has a rational element (e.g., information imbalance, competition, system risks), and irrational elements (e.g., politics, power, psychology). A logic used to link key points to sales of a company must be created by detecting the key points for each scenario type. Technical aspects such as collecting data and developing software are not major concern because they can be outsourced. The important aspect is to design an intuitive frame based on behavior principles.

Most investment companies use the method of predicting share price by adding unstructured data to leading indicators of share prices such as financial data and news. It can certainly improve the prediction, but soon competition becomes fierce. Establishing hypothesis based on behavior principles of people and programming them is most competitive in prediction. If financial and industrial indicators that do not include human behavior principles are used, the market easily changes to a red ocean (i.e., a competitive market) by Nash Equilibrium (i.e., when the information on both sides is revealed, the results create an equilibrium).

First, identify key movement (data) by understanding the types that influence share price using human behavior principles. Monitor it, create algorithms that predict the fluctuation of share price, and automate its ongoing improvement. This method is currently most effective, and more likely to remain as a blue ocean (i.e., an uncompetitive market). The reason is because this involves mostly human thinking power instead of technology.

Case Study 2
Predicting US Box Office Sales with Moving Analogy

A US box office data analytics company had requested me to provide consultation. This company provides its customers the predicted sales on the US box office through analytics and tracking. It predicts box office sales by collecting data on factors that influence box office hits in the past and applying statistical analysis, and provide the data to movie theaters and distributors for use. Specifically, it enters attributes as many times as possible for a regression equation using big data and generate results by additional processing using qualitative analysis.

This approach produced relatively accurate predictions, but had a limitation. Correlations among attributes created errors. To address this problem, I first identified the drivers that influence moviegoers. Prime examples include the number of theaters, genre, director's average sales amount, the lead actor's average sales amount, season, events, and competitiveness. Since these drivers are somewhat associated with one another, regression analysis is bound to have errors. The best approach is to use only drivers that are independent of one another, but it is difficult to select only those drivers.

Therefore, I abandoned the ordinary regression analysis prediction model, and applied a moving analogy, which predicts probabilities at a group level.

Grouping Causal Types

First, movies were grouped based on basic information for box office prediction from the distributor's point of view. The drivers used for the grouping were simple and definitive. Over 20 distinct groups were generated using the conditions that had the greatest influence (number of theaters, sales amounts for director and the lead actor, and date).

Then, viewing circumstances were grouped based on customers' viewing behavior and how movies are perceived by customers. In other words, depending on customer orientations and circumstances of movie-going, movies were classified into categories such as watching an action movie or a drama with a partner, watching a human drama with family, watching a cult movie alone. In addition, depending on how a movie was perceived, movies were positioned as summer blockbusters, horror films, and family movies.

Then, movies were classified into groups based on the basic grouping, customer type, and movie positioning. For instance, if a movie is shown in 300 to 400 theaters, average sales amounts for its director and the lead actor are $1 to $2 billion, it is released in November, and a drama for those in a relationship to spend time during weekend, it was classified as the "group 21." The number of the groups generated in this way was over 100.

Moving Analogy

1. Grouping movies from the past: For instance, if a company is predicting box office sales of a movie to be released in November 2015, group the movies that were released (and finished showing) between August 2014 and August 2015, three months prior to the time of the target movie release using the method discussed above.

2. Generation of grouping results of past movies: Generate average sales performance by group by calculating sales performance of each group (movies released in the similar condition as that of the movies in the current period).

3. Grouping the movies in the current period: Group the movies released in November 2015.

4. Prediction: Predict the sales performance of each group in November based on average sales performance by group.

This is the grouping technique, the most accurate prediction method to address the problem caused by correlations among drivers. Since this method groups customer behavior types into distinct categories and uses actual recent data, it can provide accurate data even for sales, number of people, and lasting period, etc.

Although statistical prediction can also be made using simple dummy regression analysis, accuracy suffers when attributes include those that are not dependent (e.g., sales, number of theaters, sales for actor). Therefore, in this case, moving analogy technique that employs precision grouping and analysis of sales of similar movies in similar conditions is useful.

Further Study: Permanent Customers Don't Exist

CRM Backfire

"CRM Backfire" refers to the phenomenon of companies which benefited from customer relationship management (CRM) aging and reaching a plateau as they started relying too much on CRM. This is particularly evident in the department store industry, which aggressively employed CRM. Since the 2000s, traditional department stores showed clear decline in contrast to growth of online e-commerce and outlets. One of the reasons was that large department stores failed to move beyond retaining loyal customers and ignored creating new customers as they were caught up with the promise of CRM.

CRM is basically a marketing technique that gives preferential treatment to customers with higher sales contributions. It attempts to increase sales by giving the best treatment to top customers. For this reason, in the 2000s, department stores significantly reduced the traditional mass marketing strategies of flyers and newspaper advertisements, and instead implemented promotions targeting VIP customers such as coupons, invitations to events, and family discounts. The strategy at the time was desirable for saving marketing costs and maximizing effects.

However, they overlooked the aspect of creating new customers. CRM basically excludes new customers and low-profit customers. To become a marketing target and receive VIP treatment, customers must be rated high, and thus, receive no benefits until then.

From a department store's perspective, it is more effective to market toward VIP customers than working on new customers who are uncertain at the moment. However, as time passes, young customers move to other channels before moving up to VIP class. A significant portion of new customers have already moved from department stores to global SPAs. After 10 years of CRM now, department stores are getting old with their customers. They are paying the price for focusing on existing customers only while neglecting young customers.

Brand Management

In 2014, Proctor & Gamble decided to concentrate on brand management while drastically reducing marketing positions. What is brand? It is the image of the value a product delivers to a customer. Marketing for sales only must be abandoned now. Companies must have a long-term perspective for the market, customers, and brand at the same time. Companies must strive to deliver real value to customers based on understanding of humans. They must stop watching specific customers and look at the value aspiration of the brand. The brand that "young customers always use" does not exist, but the brand that "always represents youth" does exist.

Do Not Obsess on Just Customers

Understanding customers' behavior principles has utmost significance. However, obsessing on customers per se is not the essence of a company. As companies grow larger, it becomes common that they lose important growth engines because of failing to let go of existing customers. A one-time early adopter is not an early adopter forever.

Future-oriented big data utilization is designed to improve the model while constantly evolving and use data based on value. The ultimate goal of data analytics is to deliver value to customers. Companies must exercise caution against being too focused on short-term outcomes and being bound by customers per se. Focusing on understanding the customer and aiming at future use is how one continually generates value with big data.

PART 5

What Matters at the End is Performance

CHAPTER 11

Data Is Strategy

Even Big Data Couldn't Save Sears Holdings

Sears Holdings is a global retailer which was founded in the 19th century in the US, owning stores such as Sears Department Store and Kmart. It once reigned across the US, but has currently been pushed back by competitors such as Walmart and Target, and is threatened by online retailers such as Amazon. The decline is also visible in the sales trends—its sales decreased from $50 billion in 2008 to $42 billion in 2011, in contrast to Amazon whose sales grew rapidly from $19 billion to $48 billion in the same period.

Looking for a way to fight the competition, Sears began a customer loyalty program called "Shop Your Way" in 2012. The goal of the program was to increase its loyal VIP customer base through the accumulation of data and personalized marketing. They sought to developing competitiveness through the application of the data analytics technology of its online competitor, Amazon, and a leading offline company, Tesco, to its own loyalty program.

At the time, the CTO of Sears, Phil Shelley, and the system-building team had top-class experience and knowledge in big data processing. They built the system by applying the Hadoop platform, and this Hadoop-based, big data processing system built by Sears attracted keen interest from the IT industry at the time, and was run very successfully.

First, they secured basic storage space capable of storing the data of all their customers of the past two years, improved automated processing performance by 20 to 100 times, and significantly reduced the database extraction-conversion-loading process from 10 hours to 17 minutes. They also made the system user-friendly to help those in the field create reports themselves without any IT personnel's assistance.

Did Sears actually turn the trend around? At the time, Sears became the focus of many companies' attention. Its "Shop Your Way" program appeared to have successes on the surface, such as reporting 72 percent of sales coming from loyalty membership customers.

However, this was just the effect of membership conversion of existing customers. Furthermore, by providing benefits to customers, their costs increased and store revenue decreased. Unable to find a significant difference between the program and competitors' membership programs, customers continued to ignore Sears, and sales or profits showed no distinguishable performance. In 2015, Sears closed over 200 stores, and reported an annual loss of over a billion dollars, while its share price dropped by nearly 50 percent in a year.

What went wrong? Was it too soon to see the effects of data analytics?

Separation between IT and the Field

Sears succeeded in building the system, but failed in creating a value for the customer. Sears' data analytic approach was bound to have limitations; this was because it began from the idea of "data." A big data system that does not begin from the customer will find it very difficult to create any value for the customer and the field. In the case of Sears, big data analytics did not lead to performance because the utilization technology was relatively low compared to system performance. The big data system with cutting-edge technology did no more than just recording customers' purchase information. Although countless data and various statistics were accumulated, the utilization did not go much further beyond the results of conventional, simple analysis.

Moreover, Sears' system may have been inconvenient to use offline, being appropriate only for a web environment. Hadoop distributed file systems are suitable for processing large unstructured web data; however, the offline-centered Sears had a structured database, and data properties do not vary widely enough to perform distributed processing. Its system was too technically-oriented rather than being driven by the goal of linking data to value.

In conclusion, the outcome was only a slight improvement in terms of IT. The root cause of the big data failure was the gap between the direction of the system and the utilization for marketing.

Why does this happen? Why does a company begin from data in analytics projects? The most important reason is because the problem (goal) is not clearly defined at the start, as IT and marketing is thought of as separate entities. Sears began from the vague "tool-centered" idea of trying to secure competitiveness using big data analytics and the Hadoop platform to fit the big data analytics. This strategy lost its way more and more as actual utilization proceeded. Despite expectations of finding a way forward through analyzing data, only vague ideas constantly came up, without any concrete directions for utilization.

Most companies that provide consultation on big data and sell related solutions have zero experience in solving business problems in practice. For these companies, sales are the only goal. They usually put high data processing, performance of products, and dazzling visual tools in front. Then, they advertise that big data solutions are highly effective in business, and emphasize features such as cutting-edge statistical techniques, complex algorithms, and structured reporting, distracting clients from key issues. Clients who are unfamiliar with the essence of data analytics are overwhelmed by this information and become anxious to introduce the system as soon as possible. Big data solution companies present their product as if it were a magic box that would generate the perfect solution as soon as clients put their business problem in.

However, the one who ultimately solves the problem is the client. The big data solution company's approach is like saying, "If you have a high quality instrument, you're a world-class musician." Then they leave the duty of actually playing the instrument to the client.

The Compass Called "Strategy"

The initial goal of Sears was to grow and develop competitiveness by leveraging its strengths to meet consumers' emerging needs. Sears' strengths included a traditional supplier management, an outstanding logistics system, and local customers' high recognition (brand power).

Nowadays, as consumers' economic activity areas have expanded and information delivery has become faster, in the offline retail market, only those companies that specialize in handling products for needs that can only be met offline can survive. Therefore, Sears, that was primarily an offline company, first needed to decide on its target customers for its entry to the growing market, and build a strategy to improve its stores.

For instance, the strategy could have involved making Sears' existing customers its loyal customers by emphasizing its strengths, supply and logistics, building trend-sensitive separate brand department stores with a simplified production process, and gradually evolving into the affordable supermarket that focusses on small-variety mass-production. Just these strategic directions require more effort than simply applying the "Shop Your Way" loyalty program to existing customers.

If Sears had built such strategies, it would have been able to establish hypothetical execution plans accordingly with monetization of existing loyal customers, selection of growth target customers and configuration of stores, vertical integration for small-variety mass-production, and the strategy for the trade area for entry.

Would it be possible to carry out the specific plans using data analytics? The answer is yes and no. Let us check it out by examining the execution plans one by one to see how to utilize data analytics.

1. Identify customer types by processing internal data for monetization of existing loyal customers and building CRM. Alongside identifying the customers as potential cash cows, and regularly promoting highly profitable products and their prices, establish a loyalty management system.

2. Identify growth-target customers and early adopter customers who are appropriate for the growth market in the store customer database, and configure specialized stores by conducting separate customer interviews and research.

   For instance, in the case of "small-variety mass production" stores, determine profitability based on the sales scenario by selecting price-sensitive items from the purchase database, and identifying discount-sensitive customers from the customer database.

3. Predict basic sales volume using vertical integration predictive analytics for small-variety mass-production. Then, meet with producers and discuss feasibility in detail.

4. Conduct customer segmentation to strategize the trade areas for entry, determine customer distribution using the trade area database for Sears stores, and then decide on the entry based on profitability. In the event of deciding to enter, secure an assortment of products

based on predictions on segment-specific product groups and trendy products.

According to this strategy, information on customer transactions, demographics, products, and stores must be collected first. The next stage is to process information according to the goal. For instance, if the goal is to find the answer to the question, "What are the types of purchase behavior and products of the target customers to focus primarily on in the eco-friendly market?", extract and process transaction data and demographic data using SQL (language for database inquiry). When the strategy and specific plans are established first, large-scale analysis servers or various statistical tools are often unnecessary.

Big Data and Strategy are the Best Couple

Why are primitive animals such as fish and insects still thriving without being extinct? Did dinosaurs, that ruled in the Cretaceous Period, go extinct because they were inferior? According to Charles Darwin's theory of natural selection, the creatures that survive in the world are neither the strongest nor the most intelligent. The ones that survive are the individuals that adapt to change best and have no fatal flaw.

"Van Gogh Was Ahead of His Time"

Vincent Van Gogh, a Dutch impressionist painter, created thousands of artworks throughout his life, but only one piece was sold during his lifetime. Why? Some say that the value of an artwork increases when the artist is dead, but this is just a limited interpretation. Van Gogh had an early adopter's orientation in terms of artistic style, and his work was ahead of the needs of his time. He struggled with this dilemma of whether to create commercial paintings targeted for the public to gain wealth and prestige, or to gain satisfaction with the artistic style that he wanted. He chose the latter, and as a result, it took a long time for his work to be sold commercially.

What choice should companies make to survive in the era of capitalism and competition? According to the law of evolution discussed above, they must, without a doubt, create commercially viable products. The post impressionistic work that Van Gogh wanted should never be pursued.

A company is an organism, and it finds its own way to survive instinctively. It steadily evolves by responding to changes in the environment, taking advantage of its strengths. It progresses in one single direction, whether it builds corporate strategies at a higher level, or responds to temporary situations on a short-term basis. Consequently, in most companies, the business strategy division becomes nobody's favorite because the company can manage without them even though they build ambitious strategies using complex techniques. Then, is corporate strategy essentially useless?

The reason why human beings were able to evolve into higher-level beings than chimpanzees despite similarities in their DNA is because humans made the strategic choice to use tools and raise their intellectual abilities. If they had focused only on responding to the changes in the environment at hand, they would have never given up sharp claws or walking on four limbs.

The same goes with corporate strategy. Without a strategy, a company may survive, but cannot make a quantum leap for long-term growth. Moreover, in the event of the absence of an enterprise-wide alignment of strategies (as in the case of Sears), and each division implementing an individual strategy to survive, inefficiency in the company as a whole is inevitable, and the company would fall behind.

In the contemporary world, strategy building is a must, and big data is increasingly playing a key role in this. Since strategy is conceptual and operates at a higher level, verification is important, and data analytics makes this possible. Therefore, close communication between the strategic planning team and the data analytics team is crucial, which requires experts in both areas. Data specialists must have the ability to process data to fit corporate strategy, and to communicate important information. However, such data specialists are very rare in the field, creating a bottleneck as the field of big data advances.

As previous chapters examined the principles in the utilization of data individually, this chapter discusses cases of macroscopic, data-based, corporate strategy building and execution.

Online Commerce Data Strategy Exemplified by Amazon

Amazon was founded in July 1994 to provide an internet bookstore service. Showing a monthly sales growth of 34 percent, in just a year since it launched its service, it became a worldwide sensation as an internet bookstore, and created the remarkable record of having 10 million members in 1999. In the early days, the company focused on book-buying customers, making every effort to make them loyal customers. Later, by providing Kindle—an e-book software—at a low price, Amazon encouraged ongoing e-book purchases and expanded customer traffic by providing entertainment and content services. Book-buying customers eventually became loyal customers of Amazon, and purchase areas also gradually expanded, building a solid foundation of the Amazon's growth.

As shown in the case of Amazon, the primary ingredient of success for online shopping malls is to clearly define the target customers and concentrate on them. The online shopping mall market started maturing, creating fierce competition between the players. The haphazard strategy of selling as much as possible to as many online customers as possible is likely to cause poor profitability, and hence, fail. The reason is that in the online market, the winner's curse—the winner becoming at risk or experiencing the aftermath of the win due to paying too high a price for winning—often occurs.

Many online shopping mall customers consider the entire internet as a gigantic shopping mall. Therefore, loyalty to individual websites is not very high. This is because the online environment has many "cherry-picker" customers who buy only the product that they need from one mall and leave, since they can easily move to another shopping mall with just one click.

In the offline environment, although it takes a long time to transform customer trust into loyalty, once it is built, customers do not easily move to products or services of other companies. However, in the online environment, while it is easy to attract customers, it is difficult to gain a deep trust. It is commonly seen that companies attract customers through much effort with promotions, only to let others reap the benefits due to a lack of profitability.

Therefore, "customer loyalty building" is the biggest challenge for online shopping malls. To meet this challenge, they need to make target customers loyal by concentrating resources, and securing traffic. Then, they must develop them into profitable cash-cow customers.

The first stage of the customer loyalty-building process is to identify the company's own key competencies, and determine target customers and services to concentrate on. The next stage is to secure a product assortment that fits the target customers, and run targeted promotions. Once customers build satisfactory purchase experiences through this process, they gradually become loyal customers, beginning to visit regularly.

Amazon chose book-buying customers, early adopters of online shopping at the time, as their targets. These customers not only became the key revenue source, but also helped in attracting general customers. In the case of Alibaba.com, a Chinese online shopping mall, it started with selling foreign products targeting economically capable customers who were looking for secure transactions in the then mistrusted e-commerce market. In the case of the online luxury brand, Gilt, the mall attracted trend-sensitive customers by focusing on trendy women's clothing. Most leading companies first secure their loyal target customers in this way, and then expand their products and the customer base most closely associated with the target customers.

All Customers on an Online Platform are VIPs

Amazon declared that it would create personalized shopping malls for 100 million individual customers. This meant providing shopping space optimized for each customer using data analytics. Would it be possible? It is certainly possible in the online environment, and it is also the future direction for all e-commerce companies.

The Strategy of the Platform Companies

In the past, in the offline stores, marketing (e.g., email, SMS, and mailing flyers) was conducted "outside stores" based on the results of analyzing customers' store visits and purchase histories, and personal information data. However, what is actually important is the sales activities "inside stores," which involves identifying customers' orientations and intentions, leading them to purchases, and developing them into loyal customers when they visit the stores. Unfortunately, it is difficult for data analytics to be truly effective offline because it has not been possible to program responses to customers in stores. It is difficult in practice to manualize the response-approach specific to a customer type and train staff accordingly.

The best part of utilizing data analytics for online shopping malls is the ability to generate customized responses in real time based on algorithms. In the online environment, one-on-one response to customers is possible. The analytic technology these days can even check the time that a customer spent reading a page, and the movement pattern of a mouse, and convert these into data. The system can identify customer behavior from the moment he or she enters the online shopping mall and implement the algorithm accordingly; this is like placing sales robots in charge of work in a shopping mall.

Example: Customer Management at an Offline Department Store

Cheryl is a VIP customer of a department store. One day, she visited the department store as usual. She used the familiar valet parking and went up to the women's clothing department on the second floor. She then visited the fashion brand store managed by Judy, whom she had become close to, and had a lively conversation with her.

Judy is a veteran manager who has managed Cheryl as a customer for 15 years, and she even knows Cheryl's family businesses, personal orientations, and personality. Judy became familiar with Cheryl's favorite fashion styles and colors, and when new products Cheryl might like come in, Judy calls Cheryl to let her know and invites her for a look-around, while checking how she's doing. Probably enjoying Judy's approach, Cheryl frequently chatted with Judy and developed their relationship, while responding to the manager's calls or texts with excitement. She gradually became Judy's VIP customer, and developed into a loyal customer of the department store and the brand.

In general, when responding to a customer, the manager, Judy, identifies the customer's orientation and intention. When the customer, Cheryl, visits, Judy greets her, asks how she is doing, and asks what brought her to the store. If Cheryl's visit is just to enjoy some company while having a coffee, Judy offers a casual chat in a comfortable environment. The customer then looks around the clothes casually and leaves.

If the customer, Cheryl, is looking for an outfit to wear at her relative's wedding in the weekend, Judy makes relevant suggestions. If Cheryl wants to buy an outfit for her nephew as his birthday present, Judy asks about the nephew's tastes and preferences and makes relevant suggestions. If Cheryl indicates the need for a new formal outfit for the upcoming season, Judy shows her the clothes that match well with her fashion style and existing clothes, and makes a sale after some pleasant talk.

This example illustrates the VIP sales process that occurs in an offline retail store. In the offline environment, sales associates develop relationships with customers and build trust in face-to-face situations. Sales associates become familiar with clients' tastes, preferences, and characteristics naturally. Relationships with customers become stronger, and customers do not leave the store that easily.

Can such offline sales approaches also be created online? Yes. As mentioned earlier, by recognizing customer's orientations and intentions, and creating the corresponding algorithm, online shopping malls can also make VIP sales personalized to individual customers as in the offline environment.

Algorithm Automation Technique for Online Shopping Malls

The process of a customer's visit to and behavior at an online shopping mall can broadly be divided into six stages. For each stage, an algorithm for personalized management, like the approach to department store VIP customers, is created and operated.

Organizing the First Screen

Generally, immediately after the launch of a shopping mall, the proportion of indirect inflow through sites such as banner ads, portals, and price comparison sites, is higher than that of direct inflow such as URL, favorites, and keyword search. However, to develop these visitors into loyal customers, the direct inflow must grow gradually. The key to direct inflow is to build customer trust by providing satisfaction. Then, the customer recognizes the shopping mall as a playground to look around and play at will, and begins to visit it directly.

In general, customers visit the shopping mall directly when they have 3.6 satisfactory shopping experiences on an average (with variations across product types). An accumulation of satisfactory experiences means that the following two messages have been conveyed to the customer. First, the shopping mall "has an assortment of products or offers that fit me (there is no need to go to other shopping malls)," and second, the mall "often has new products and fun events (come and play more often)." If these two are satisfied, the customer considers that it is worth visiting directly, and the traffic increases.

The organization of the first screen for a customer's visit to the online shopping mall involves, first of all, suggesting products that are personalized to the customer. A department store's sales manager determines a customer type intuitively after having a few conversations with the customer. Then, the manager responds accordingly to that particular customer type skillfully, and gradually uses a precisely personalized approach.

The same applies to the online mall. First, an inference on the customer's type is made based on customer characteristics, and then the site makes a suggestion of personally related products and product sets specific to the customer's type. Once the suggested products are decided on, key points are determined and delivered. Different types of customers have different points that catch their eyes. Elements that attract a customer's attention include brands, designs, and wording. The screen is organized to showcase these points, and optimized using the AB test (present the customer with Page A and Page B at random, and choose the page that receives a better response).

The customer is presented with a sensitive offer on the first screen. It is inefficient to present all customers with discount coupons through a pop-up window. The key to online sales is to offer absolutely necessary offers. Offers such as sales points, limited time offer, and giveaways must be selectively provided by identifying the customer's orientation, like how department store sales associates prepare giveaways that a VIP customer is likely to appreciate. Regarding the method, the system must identify pain points at the customer purchase stage based on the customer profiling discussed earlier, and deliver the offer that addresses these.

Visit Intention Analysis and Response

Human beings do not always behave mechanically following their orientations. Customers have different intentions when visiting a shopping mall depending on the situation. Although it is a must to respond to a customer based on orientation using customer profiling, recognizing the customer's intention and responding to it is a different challenge.

When a VIP customer visits a store at a department store, the sales manager determines the customer's visit intention through a conversation after a brief greeting. The manager determines whether the customer is just window shopping, or is looking for a product for a present, or is comparing new products, or if the customer is ready to purchase. The manager then responds accordingly. The realization of this process online involves defining intention types, intention identification modeling, and performing type-specific response modeling.

1. Defining intention type: First, define hypothetical "intention types," and verify them using basic survey and interviews. Customer's intentions include window shopping, comparison of options, deciding to purchase, and purchasing for others. Intention types must have clearly differentiated behavior patterns, be readable in data, and be able to generate meaningful responses from the site. Classify intentions into types that can be designed.

2. Intention identification modeling: Identify behaviors for each type and detect them in data. In the online environment, it is impossible to ask a customer about his or her visit intention as a sales associate can do at a department store. Therefore, identify the intention based on the customer's behavior on the first screen of the online shopping mall (first click). To do this, a clear clue that can capture the intention in the customer's behavior must be identified.

For instance, if a customer uses a product keyword such as "swimsuit" when searching for products, this can be interpreted as the customer having little background knowledge on specific brands or specific features, and the intention to find products with a mass appeal. If a female customer searches a keyword such as "men's jacket," or "gift," this can be considered as an intention to buy a present for her spouse or friend. If a customer clicks on a food or a gift set category on the menu during the holiday season, it can be considered as an intention for a large-scale holiday purchase, and if a female customer clicks on an event banner or a new product, it can be interpreted as a window shopping intention.

It is necessary to define the rule to detect each intention type in this process, and program it into an algorithm to determine intentions.

3. Type-specific response modeling: Once the intention is determined, make a real-time response. If the intention is a one-time gift, ignore existing shopping patterns. Suggest items for gifts and related products, and assist the customer with gathering information by offering sensitive offers in order to encourage purchase decision. If the intention is determined as the need for household products after a recent moving, suggest moving-related products such as TVs, stereos, dining tables, and decoration items, and encourage large purchases. For the set of suggested products, identify them in advance using data analytics, and program it to respond according to the intention in real time.

Assisting Information Exploration

Many online shopping mall customers spend a lot of time in information exploration. Customers never move on to the next stage unless they feel that they have exhausted all the information on the product they want to purchase by exploring information. Therefore, the most important goal of this stage is to "lead the customer to finish information exploration and move on to the next stage (purchase decision)."

In the approach to VIP customers, sales managers at a department store usually choose and show customers only a few products that the customers are likely to like because they know the customers' styles. The secret is that sales managers have dealt with many VIP customers, and have knowledge on the products that such customers prefer. The managers have the entire map of customers' favorite products in their heads.

Realization of this online is the real-time related product suggestions. The online malls show a set of the best products related to the products on the page the customer visits. The reason for suggesting related products is because customers can move on to the next stage (purchase decision) only after seeing the entire set of the products (moreover, revenue can be generated using personalized ads based on the features of related products).

In addition, the sites can accelerate the behavior stage using personalized offers. That is, they can identify the pain points for specific customers (usually the customer type who has some difficulty in making a purchase decision) to encourage them to skip information exploration and purchase decision steps. When a sales manager says, "This is the last one left for this size," or "Today is the last day of the sale," it helps customers skip the stages of information exploration and purchase decision by delivering the message that "Don't worry because this product is a popular product," or that "It's your loss if you miss this chance."

To implement this online may involve providing a specific customer type (difficulty with purchase decision) with a "limited-time discount offer," or indicating "impending sold out (number of inventory)" to encourage a purchase decision.

Inducing Purchase Decision and Additional Purchase

Customers move on to the purchase decision stage and put products in the shopping cart. The shopping cart content reveals the shopping purpose. When a customer puts many products in the shopping cart as in the online supermarket, additional purchases can be induced by identifying the shopping purpose. If the previous stage made a rough guess on the visit intention, this stage can identify a customer's specific shopping purpose.

As the number of products in the cart grows, the purpose becomes clearer. A specific shopping purpose can be identified regarding whether the customer wants to buy "products needed for holiday-home visits," "products needed as season changes," or "wedding products."

Once the purpose is identified, induce additional purchases. For each purpose, the list of products to purchase is already established. In this case, related products can be sold additionally, or purchase benefits for over a certain amount can be offered to induce additional spending. Organize a related product set optimized for each shopping cart (shopping purpose); then, respond accordingly in real time.

Satisfaction Management

This is the approach at the stage when a customer makes a payment for a product. This is the stage that gives customers the experience of "satisfactory shopping." In general, sales managers at department stores give out benefits gained from this purchase to VIP customers. For instance, they increase customer satisfaction and gain trust by helping them at the payment stage with a gift card or by informing them on how to use coupons.

The online shopping malls basically take an approach tailored to customer type. While price-insensitive customers are not sensitive to coupons, for price-sensitive customers, it is important to gain trust by promoting coupons. For instance, the payment page can show "available points" and "coupons" at the bottom, in a prominent way. Moreover, gifts or point can be provided or their membership class can be upgraded to increase satisfaction and develop them into loyal customers.

When coupons and points are unused, the company's revenue increases in the short term, but it does not help in the long run. According to results of analytics, revenues from unused coupons are lower than the effect of increased customer satisfaction and the sales increase generated by coupon use.

Inducing revisit of new customers is very important. From my experience, visiting a shopping mall three times a month was a major sign of loyal customers. Therefore, for new customers, promotions like coupons that expire in two weeks are effective.

Loyalty Management

The previous stages are the approaches needed when a customer is logged into the online shopping mall. However, continuing loyalty management is necessary when the customer logs out of the shopping mall. In the case of department store sales manages, they conduct customized management for VIP customers by maintaining relationships through making calls and sending texts on a regular basis, and personalized management such as sending hand-written letters.

The same applies to online shopping malls. Manage all customers precisely according to the pain points based on customer profiling. Send emails and texts to customers who are in need of information, and inform customers sensitive to discounts of sales offers. If the company owns multiple types of stores, induce omni-channel purchases depending on the needs of the channel.

Many companies waste a large number of promotions by sending them to unspecified, large numbers of customers. Their mindset is that since the media to access customers such as texts, emails, mails, and push alerts on their smartphones are not very costly, it is okay to send them in bulk randomly.

Most marketing personnel think of sending out promotions from a cost perspective. However, let us think from a customer's point of view. If they receive unnecessary information continuously, customers become stressed out, and develop a negative image of that medium and of the company.

Customers respond to promotions in the following four ways: "actively exploring," "passive," "bothered," and "negative"; the "bothered" and "negative" customer groups attempt to unsubscribe when unsatisfactory experiences occur 3.3 times in a row on average. In other words, the chance to approach the customer is only 3.3 times, and the company must deliver a satisfactory experience for that particular medium within 3.3 times.

This requires delivery of sensitive information at the right time using a precise medium. Deliver it by personalizing for individual customers the medium, offers, and content that customers are sensitive to, and in the case of a medium that cannot be personalized such as regular mails, organize the content by categorizing the groups. It is important to establish a system for automated production and to send them out based on the customer profiling and clustering results discussed earlier.

As seen above, it is necessary to optimize through conducting the AB tests continuously even after configuring the online shopping mall according to stage-specific approaches. When the company is too focused on the up and down movement of total sales, it often fails to determine which stage a problem occurs in. Therefore, it must clearly define the outcome for each stage (e.g., whether customers moved on to the next stage, made additional clicks), and keep making modifications toward higher outcomes using the AB test. The online shopping mall requires ongoing management and changes, since it is also the space that a living and breathing customer uses.

In the online environment, the success of the shopping mall hinges upon the sophistication of its response to customers when they visit the site. Increasing value by taking into account each and every type of behavior of customers living in the online era is the task that data analysts must take on.

Case Study
Big Data Strategy for Convenience Stores

Convenience stores (CVS) are emerging as a major retail spot, doing more than simply meeting needs for getting necessities or food locally. This occurs because, as the product delivery process is increasingly simplified to the "producer-logistics-consumer" process due to changes in online businesses and innovations in logistics, convenience stores are at the forefront of being contact points with consumers. CVSs will become an important channel for meeting all local needs most responsively.

Building CVS business strategies requires an examination of customer behavior principles first. Understanding customer types must precede and be used for analysis of the local trade areas. Customer and store analysis methods based on data analytics can be divided into the following three steps.

Analysis 1. Customer Profiling and Clustering

Identify customer orientation attributes based on CVS customer behavior and purchased products using internal data, and perform customer profiling. Small retail stores such as CVSs are characteristically poor in recognizing customers (e.g., it is still uncommon for a customer to present a membership card when buying cigarettes at CVS). Records on purchases exist, but it is unknown who made the purchases. Therefore, in this case, customer orientations must be analyzed based on the data from a small number of recognized customers (later, backtrack to the distribution of individual customer types using purchase records of individual CVSs).

Then, classify customer types by clustering the customer profiling results statistically. For instance, the CVS with a trade area of a residential area may have customer types of "men living alone in a studio who purchase precooked food" or "high school girls living in apartments who purchase snacks." The CVS with a trade area of a subway station may have customer types of "office workers who primarily buy cigarettes and beverages," or "college students who buy beverages and cosmetic products."

Analysis 2. Distribution Analysis of Customers within a Trade Area

Once types of customers of all CVSs are determined, identify the characteristics and types of individual CVSs based on the customer types. As mentioned earlier, the proportion of CVS customers that can be recognized is very low, at below 10 percent. Therefore, determine the distribution of types of recognized customers for each CVS. Then, estimate the types of the all recognized and unrecognized customers based on the recognized customer distribution and sales of the CVS.

Next, complement the trade area customer distribution using the store's sales data (e.g., sold product groups, brands, prices, volumes, and times of sale) and statistical data for respective areas (e.g., gender, age, economic ability). Each customer type has preferred product groups and brands, and the purchase time and day of week that differ from other types. It is necessary to modify the results on customer type distribution based on the differences among customer types.

Analysis 3. Store Profiling, Clustering, and Understanding

Profile stores using three types of data—distribution of customer types, competitions, and area statistics—and perform clustering using the profiles (see Analysis 1 for distribution of customer types).

Competitions in the trade area are analyzed based on the data on competing retail stores around the CVS. CVSs do not compete with other CVSs only. They also compete with kiosks, large supermarkets, and even department stores. Competitions can be determined using sales data. First, define competing products, and generate a competitiveness index based on the differences in the average sales data of similar stores.

Area statistics are defined based on the trade area of general real estate, and include gender ratio, age distribution, and income. Types of trade areas include weekend, business day, office, shopping, special events, and residential trade areas.

Once stores are clustered into types, identify the characteristics of each type (as in customer personal analysis), and the needs of its trade area.

If the basic model of customer and store analysis is created through the above process, it can be used for business strategies. In the following section, let us examine the applications of data analytics.

Application 1. Strategy for Competitive Market Profitability

First, analyze whether the market is a competitive or monopolistic market, based on the trade area of the store. The strategy would vary depending on the competitive relations.

Example: Customer Behavior in the Competitive Market

"Mike works at a company near Brooklyn. In the area, there are three CVSs, and by regularly buying basic sandwiches and beverages from CVSs, Mikes came to know the types and prices of sandwiches sold in all three of the CVSs from purchase experiences. For over a year, Mike has been using the CVS that sells his favorite sandwich at the lowest price."

In the competitive market, customers have many choices when they have needs for CVS, and are willing to visit a CVS based on comparison of CVSs and supermarkets located within 150 ft. on average from the routes they usually use. Therefore, in the competitive market, it is most important to win the competition by coming up with the most competitive products and the prices that customers usually make comparisons on.

Individual customers have high-involvement products (key comparison products that show their preferences clearly) and low-involvement products (products they are little concerned with and are hence insensitive about differences). Therefore, in the competitive area, a CVS must draw customers in by winning in the competition for high-involvement products, and raise profit by selling low-involvement products additionally. In the case of Mike, he visits CVSs for sandwiches (price-sensitive product), and buys other products such as cigarettes and beverages (price-insensitive products) additionally.

Example: Customer Behavior in the Monopolistic Market

"Lauren who lives in Queens occasionally visits CVSs to buy snacks and beverages. There is a CVS at a 3-minute walking distance from her home, and because the other CVS is at a 10-minute walking distance, she does not even think about going to other CVS. Lauren likes snacks and beverages at the CVS, and sometimes buys daily products or beer and snacks from there on her way home. Even though she has lived for over 5 years in this area, she has never made comparisons of CVSs in the area."

In the case of the monopolistic market, the only concern for a customer when he or she has a need for a CVS is "whether to buy or not." The only competitor in the monopoly is the customer's wallet. The best strategy is to consider how much customers are willing to pay, and price the product at the highest possible price within the range. Therefore, the monopolistic market strategy is focused on maximizing profits. It is important to generate the optimal price for each product that maximizes sales and profit by estimating customers' price sensitivity.

Application 2. Optimization of Store-Specific Marketing

Establish the marketing strategies for each store based on the distribution of store types and customer types generated earlier. First, analyze CVS visit and purchase behavior of individual customer types using interviews and observations. Then, determine pain points by identifying the difficulties customers have. In conclusion, find a way to address the pain points and establish marketing strategies accordingly.

For instance, the company can send information to the customers who have needs for inexpensive mobile phones but are unaware that they can buy them in the CVS, or provide the customers who are sensitive to discounts with membership mileage better than the nearby supermarket.

The strategies may employ the non-system approach (e.g., changes in shelf configuration, product composition, and display) or the system approach (e.g., SMS or mailing to customers).

Example: CVS A

- Store cluster: Store focused on affordable daily products for small families
- Competition: Competition index of 30 (one mid-sized supermarket within 100m distance)

Customer Type 1: Young Woman in a One-Person Household

- Purchase behavior: Chooses high-quality food products, and low-priced beverages. Purchases basic medical products and periodically purchases pantyhose and electrical products (e.g., light bulbs).
- Pain point: Unaware that "CVS sells fresh, high quality food."
- Marketing strategy: Send SMS with a list of "best products for one-person household," and display fresh food products on the commuting hours.

Customer Type 2: Man with Children

- Purchase behavior: Frequently purchases cigarettes and beverages, and occasionally purchases packaged foods and office products.
- Pain point: Being sensitive to prices of beverages and food, but little knowledge of prices of other products.
- Marketing strategy: Calculate price sensitivity for beverages and food products, make the price of price-sensitive products

10 percent lower than those of competitors, and price the price-insensitive products to maximize profit.

Application 3. New Product Development Based on Customer Needs

"Find the product that customers want but the store does not have."

Discover the product that is necessary for customers (i.e., likely to be sold), but that the store does not have currently. Set it as a goal to constantly find and put in place what customers need in everyday life. Regarding the product to sell, make a prediction based on customer distribution in the trade area.

1. Create a list of predicted sales products based on distribution of customer types in the trade area. The predicted sales volume for each product can be obtained by generating the rankings of the products customers are interested in and multiplying them by the number of residents in the area.
2. Procure the products that are on the predicted sales product list, but not in the store (test it using a short-term pilot sale).
3. Regularly create the best product portfolio based on customer composition and store size.

Application 4. Prediction of Hit Product and Taking Action

Create a system for CVS hit product prediction for quick response.

1. Identify the trend-sensitive customer type and the trend-sensitive trade area.
2. Collect data on product and brand trends using major online sites.
3. Calculate repurchase rate of the trend-sensitive customer group.
4. Predict the sales flow for the coming six months using regression analysis.
5. Develop the PB products identical to trendy products and expand supplies.

Application 5. Strategy for Entry to Trade Areas

Build the trade area entry strategy based on customer distribution and the number of people passing by.

1. Create a database on customer distribution and competitions for individual trade areas of the northeastern region of the US (external data collection).
2. Designate the optimal type of CVSs for each trade area using the database on CVS types built earlier.
3. Conduct a simulation to predict customer inflow and sales (2).
4. Decide whether to enter the area based on the prediction about the future financial statement for the coming five years.

These application strategies can be used by most local retail stores. The system built in this process self-grows as the number of recognized customers grows.

How to Defeat Amazon

Amazon's personalized shopping mall approach is the best large online retail approach currently available that combines the platform and relevant algorithms. Amazon has the algorithm for identifying customer needs sensitively and making suggestions, which is primarily based on the results of analysis on customers' purchase history and product views. Though the behavior analytics still need improvement, they are still more advanced than those used by their competitors.

So can this approach satisfy all customers by providing "100 million optimized shopping malls for 100 million customers" as Amazon intended? The answer is probably 'no.' Just like how no matter how much a bottle can be packed with pebbles, it still has empty spaces where sand can fit in, in the same way, no matter how well a single platform can be personalized, it cannot meet all needs that customers have.

Humans are not just rational beings that an algorithm can predict or analyze. It is possible to make suggestions of optimized products for individual customers and group them based on algorithms; however, customers have distinct tastes such as design, fonts, configuration of menu, and contents, in the process starting from the click on the first screen, to browsing and making payments, as well as that of choosing products. One cannot meet the needs of all customers in terms of preferences and tastes using the single platform of Amazon.com.

Let us take a look at Amazon's fashion retail. Its open market shopping mall for the general public is "Amazon Fashion." However, Amazon also has additional shopping mall sites with distinct tastes such as Zappos, Shopbop, East Dane, and MyHabit. If Amazon was able to provide everyone with an optimized shopping mall using "Amazon Fashion," these independent sites would not have been necessary. However, it was difficult to have the assortment and atmosphere that would fit fashion customers with distinctive personalities with only the platform of "Amazon Fashion." A similar example is Instagram of Facebook, an independent space with superior photo features to enhance the network and increase traffic for customers with clear preferences for photo sharing.

Divide the Market

Every product group has two types of customers—the general public and value-seeking customers. In the case of online shopping malls, the general public, who are relatively uninterested in fashion, purchase inconspicuous, affordable, regular products from "Amazon Fashion." However, value-seeking customers who are very interested in fashion actively search for products and malls that fit their tastes (in terms of offline stores, it can be understood as how Uniqlo targets the general public, and SOHO stores target value seekers). Having achieved a rapid growth with regular products in the early days, Amazon had difficulty in catering to value seekers, and recognized the limitations of a single platform. Consequently, the company began to acquire shopping sites with distinct styles.

The reason for the recent surge in sales of unique fashion shopping malls is because the needs of value seekers, that large online stores cannot meet, are increasing. Online fashion customers initially used large online stores, but as they gained more online shopping experience, they sought fashion shopping malls that fit their needs. Small fashion shopping malls that catered to such needs were able to solidify their positioning in the market, and grew into large companies.

The successful operation of online stores has two important aspects: the first is to create a dynamic platform to provide suggestions and perform promotions optimized for the general public as in "Amazon Fashion," and the second is to provide an independent space customized for value-seeking customers as in "Zappos."

To summarize, the way to defeat Amazon is to realize customer optimization with a large platform, or carve out the market by creating an independent site catered to the needs of individual customer types.

Compete in the Growing Market

It is now the era of platform war. Controlling customer traffic is the topmost priority. However, in the existing markets with established camps, competitors have a strong defense against one another. Since no one is willing to give in to others, it will eventually become a zero-sum game.

Therefore, the best way to expand the company is to jump into the growing market and declare ownership. In most industries, companies implement such a strategy to control the growing market when they try to reverse the power balance. That is, companies secure loyal customers and traffic by taking a lead in the growing market. As of the mid-2010s, a variety of growing markets exist including mobiles, luxury fashion, silver industry, online fresh food, and Chinese goods. Companies must develop a keen eye to identify growing markets, and expand their platforms.

There are two ways to identify growing markets. First, companies can check the 'click and search' data of their websites and figure out how many clicks happen and how many purchases were made for each product. The conversion rate can be calculated from the purchase amount divided by the click amount; the 'lost opportunity' can then be calculated from the average conversion rate and product conversion rate. A product or brand with a high 'lost opportunity' can be identified as the growing market. In the same way, we can check search keywords. If there are not any products/ brands that show up with high lost opportunity keywords, those are the first products companies should source and provide to our customers.

A second way to find the growing market is by obtaining statistics via collecting and analyzing external big data, predicting hit products or brands using internal data, predicting growing categories, and discovering empty markets (qualitative investigation must also accompany this).

In addition, in the early days, it is important to secure traffic by creating a playground for target customers using curation for the growing market.

CEOs who fail often make the error of being passive when investment is necessary, while investing when investment is unnecessary. It must be kept in mind that the way to defeat Amazon is to continuously monitor growing markets and meet customers' needs. If this is followed, at some point, the company will take over the market.

Is Uber an Illusion—Shared Economy and Big Data

The N (Network) generation refers to those who were born between 1977 and 1997, and who are highly skilled in handling digital devices. The N generation engages in two-way instead of one-way communication using the internet, and wants to be active users instead of passive viewers.

The S (Social media) generation refers to those who were born in 1997 or later. The S generation is better at collaboration and sharing than previous generations and seeks fun and speed. Moreover, they solve various problems, have interpersonal relationships, and reveal personalities on various platforms simultaneously, view the world from platforms such as Facebook and Google, and utilize them as part of their cognitive domains.

These characteristics of the N and the S generations exist because they live in the era of material and information overload. Since they are highly capable of choosing the information they want from among a massive amount of information, they know how to use active data platforms well.

Obsessed with growth since the Industrial Revolution, humanity has made tremendous growth continuously. As a result, supply has surpassed demands since the 2000s, and now more than what humanity needs is produced.

However, this oversupply does not lead to materialistic abundance. The problems in distribution still exist due to the problems in the social systems and inconsistent information. In other words, the demand-supply imbalance, in which demands are not generated due to a lack of information, and as a result, supply is not provided, still clearly exists.

The currently emerging "shared economy business" such as Uber, Zipcar, and Airbnb started from the efforts that were taken to address this problem. Transportation information services such as Uber, Zipcar, and shared parking are simple information sharing systems that connect cars that are currently not in use with customers who want to use them at a low cost. The growth of these service markets indicates that there is a high need for low-cost and sharing-based services. The ownership concept is increasingly reduced, and the business for rentals is expanding. Although a very simple idea, shared business is becoming real due to the emergence of the S generation and the growth of smartphones.

The current shared economy is currently just providing platform services for sharing information on demand and supply among those with the goal of sharing. Then, what would the next stage of platforms look like? It would look like choosing, processing, and delivering the demand-supply information according to customer needs.

Airbnb—Just an Information Sharing Site?

Airbnb is an online site that provides service for renting a part of a residence to others. As of 2013, it was broking 35,000 accommodations in 192 countries. The market estimated the company value of Airbnb as $13 billion. This is higher than the total current value of a large hotel company such as Hyatt.

In the traditional online accommodation and travel service market, companies such as Expedia and Orbitz provided accommodation and flight reservation services by working with hotels and serviced residences. However, in addition to commercial hotels, there are countless, unused, so-called "vacant" residences, and there are needs to use them at low costs. Airbnb provided an online space to exchange information freely between those suppliers who have these vacant accommodations and those consumers who look for affordable accommodations. This platform brought to the surface the needs for travel and leisure which used to be suppressed for economic reasons, and thanks to users' enthusiastic responses, Airbnb expanded the platform and continued to grow.

The high value of shared economy companies such as Airbnb is based on the future growth factor. The market forecasts that Airbnb, a leading accommodation and travel platform, will have a huge customer base and dominate hotel-based giant competitors. This is because Airbnb communicates with customers with accumulated transaction data, and expand business areas as they are constantly developing individually optimized services.

Airbnb is planning on gradually providing comprehensive personalized services covering accommodation and all travel services including suggesting optimized destinations and providing promotions. This is an evolution of services to identifying and satisfying individual needs (e.g., desire to travel, anxiety regarding missing discount opportunities) based on customer data analytics.

As shown in the case of Airbnb, just sharing information on the platform can generate a high value in today's materially-overloaded society. The future direction of the platform utilization will inevitably be to identify customers' needs and connect precise information through data analysis.

Further Study: Platform of Happiness

"One day, Amelie found someone a photo with a memory of 50 years ago by chance, and the owner of the photo was deeply moved by this small act of kindness. Witnessing this, Amelie starting to make people happy and give them a dream and hope with a variety of abilities. Although the abilities were not particularly special and were just to stage situations, people began to experience happiness in the situations."—*Amelie* (2001)

Data Platform for Providing Happiness

As discussed earlier, the essence of data analytics is to identify and satisfy customer needs. As the era of utilization and sharing begins, views on service is shifting from "wealth" itself to the value that humans gain from the service, namely, the "happiness" services.

Major trends of future technical services can be classified into the following three types.

First, using technology ranging from smartphones to wearable devices to ubiquitous computing, people will be able to get information without the restriction of time and space.

Second, people will be presented the best possible services based on data about their sense of happiness (instead of a material basis) and they will actively enjoy the services. Rather than just giving happiness, the services can provide sense of community through "expansion of experiences" by experiencing a variety of lives.

Third, with the advances in robot technology and machine learning technology, the most important ability for humans will be the ability to enjoy the work they want to do, rather than the ability to perform well.

In summary, in the future, data utilization will continue to present the direction toward experiencing the most happiness and creating various ways of happiness constantly based on analysis of information of individuals. Moreover, instead of individually separate services, an integrated personalized platform will be created by integrating aspects of occupation, hobby, family, friends, travel, eating out, shopping, and medical services. This platform will serve as an organic system that controls long-term demands and supplies.

This "happiness platform" can also be programed based on data analytics, and the approach is not different from the existing method. The only difference is to shift the direction from "maximizing profits" to "maximizing happiness." Let us take a closer look at this process.

First, categorize the ways that people usually experience happiness, determine the process hypothetically using interviews and surveys, and identify them in the database as much as possible. For instance, if you selected the attribute of "getting a sense of accomplishment from decorating home interiors," identify the signs of purchasing related materials and assembling and installing items at home in the database. Then, verify the results on the happiness gained from the attribute, using data such as online group activities, photos on parties with relatives, and health signs (measure them when the amount of data grows, and in the early stages, utilize the data on information services that customers agree to receive).

As the countless patterns of gaining happiness are identified, their antecedents and consequences can be detected using deep analysis technique. Identify behaviors (to find happiness) using data, and profile them by indexing them. This will allow identification and utilization of individually-specific happiness gaining points.

Once individuals are clustered based on profiles, people with similar orientations in finding happiness are grouped together. The platform can generate the effect of collective intelligence by providing type-specific information for happiness-seeking or happiness-promoting individuals to get together and create a community and exchange information.

Build a sustainable platform through exchanges with other communities and new happiness attributes so that the sense of happiness continues to grow for individuals and types. However, clustering can make people stick to the cluster, blocking a move to another dimension of happiness. Therefore, we should allow people to find happiness using ways such as Facebook friend suggestion feature (exchanging various types of friends periodically, and suggest using the quantum jump-type of approach). This is how the experience can be expanded with a paradigm shift, and can develop a sense of community by exchanging various experiences.

CHAPTER 12

Big Data—A Long Way to Go

The Fall of Data Elites

The Battle of Guandu is one of three battles in Chinese *Three Kingdoms* and an important battle between Cao Cao and Yuan Shao. The battle was won by Cao Cao. However, no one expected him to win because Yuan Shao had the most powerful force at the time.

Being from a prestigious family and backed by numerous powerful figures, Yuan Shao was ready to rule the world after completing the elite course. Moreover, Yuan Shao's force was 700,000 large and 10 times as big as Cao Cao's force and unlikely to be defeated. What brought Yuan Shao down to his knee?

In the Battle of Guandu, Yuan Shao was defeated by Cao Cao in a single battle. With the intelligence that Yuan Shao's food supplies were kept in the Wuchao, Cao Cao raided the army supply station with his 5000 infantry and light infantry men, completely destroying the supply guard troops and burning the food supply. Despite having the enormous force, advanced weapons, strong generals, and outstanding strategists, Yuan Shao's force was defeated and had to retreat without having a decent fight. It was extremely unfortunate from Yuan Shao's perspective. Despite having everything necessary for winning a battle, he lost because of the problem that he did not consider a big deal (namely, food). This led Yuan Shao's force to a complete fall.

Why does big data fail? Data analytics does not always succeed when it has all requirements for success (e.g., creating value, precise data processing, and strategic use) met. According to my experience, data analytics often fails when it is so close to a win because of external factors rather than data analytics itself. Errors in the execution process and organizational issues often work as obstacles.

As demonstrated in Yuan Shao's defeat, despite near perfection, missing one in the execution process can lead to a defeat (and for this reason, many mistrust data analytics). While basic activities of companies (e.g., sales, production, logistics) translates into results that are as much as the inputs made, strategic activities commonly result in dichotomous outcomes of either success or failure. Despite perfect design of data analytics and utilization model, all efforts of data analytics sometimes end up being in vain due to a single minor error in judgment in the execution process.

Let us go over the case of Tesco that we discussed earlier. What was the reason for Tesco to have difficulty in global expansion? The reason was that Tesco was careless in the middle process that connects data analytics to outcomes. It made the error of applying the existing data analytics model to other countries.

In the emerging markets, Tesco was literally an elite. In the eyes of the local companies, which were busy making sales haphazardly through unsystematic approaches such as improvised sales, Tesco appeared to be the elite group that brought in the magic box called state-of-the-art data analytics system from the UK and carried out marketing planning with no difficulty.

However, the barrier in the real life was surprisingly high. The non-localized analytics-based marketing plans could not be implemented, and were left unused. Foreign countries had completely different market environments such as marketing process, organization of headquarters, and partnering organizations.

No matter how sophisticated an analytic system is, it is unlikely to be effective without the support of the process and organization. Tesco needed to optimize the execution process through collaboration with local suppliers, marketing agencies, and system companies. Most of all, it needed to have changed its outlook as the analytic marketing team blended in with the existing organization. In general, a company's implementation arms lack flexibility due to the focus on immediate profit. Unless the data analytics team makes strong efforts to work together with others in the organization, instead of dominating others, the project is bound to fail.

As data technology becomes increasingly complex and difficult for laymen to understand, the gap between building and executing big data-based strategies grows in companies. This big data strategy—how should we implement it?

Maturity of Collective Consciousness

If Apple's iPhone came out 20 years ago, would it have been successful? It would not. It's because the market was not ready to accept it. Collective cognitive level of consumers and manufacturers in the period determines demand and supply.

The same applies to the corporate strategies driven by big data. Big data in the current times is a very specialized field and challenging to even the CEOs with high intellect. Integration of such big data analytics into the company and producing results hinges on the collective consciousness of the management and personnel in various divisions, and requires company-wide consensus on data analytics. Implementation is possible only when everyone understands and collaborates. However, many people have a preconception that big data is difficult. People will not implement something if they do not understand it. As a result, most companies do not go further than just consulting the results of data analytics.

It is not advised to force people to use the results of big data analytics. Analysts must present technology according to maturity of collective consciousness. The leadership must go together instead of going alone in the front

Data Analytics—Never Be Superior

People listen not to those who are right but to those they are close to. It is the same with companies. Ignoring those in other divisions and forcing them to use data analytics reports in their work is a shortcut to failure. While everyone involved must make efforts to understand data analytics, the role of data analysts is more important than others.

Data analytics is a total art. As an orchestra conductor must be able to play all instruments well, it is very important for data analysts to understand and adjust the level to the divisions that use the results. It is much easier for data analysts to present the results of analytics from the perspective of the divisions than for the divisions (e.g., sales, production, procurement) to understand the data analysts' perspective. Most data analysts consider this work a chore, but it is an essential task for them to take on.

Three Rules for Achieving Results

It is not recommended to obsess over doing good data analytics. It is certainly good to do it well, but it must be kept in mind that it is far more important to link analytics to results. This requires performance-oriented project management. That is, abandon the part that does not give results and take charge of and finish the part that produces results. The activity to remove obstacles to execution is required. This is because many obstacles exist between data analytics and actual results, as mentioned earlier.

The following describes the three stages of eliminating the obstacles in realizing the results of big data analytics. Although it is impossible to apply these to all companies in the same way, I encourage you to take the following suggestions to develop the insight to assess if data analytics will generate results and to connect data analytics to results.

First, keep the execution process as simple as possible. Because it is difficult to determine what went wrong where in the process when applying modeling (analytics results program) to reality in data analytics, errors are often missed. The data analytics utilization process has key strategic points such as development delivery, system performance, personnel understanding, and supplier agreement. These points must be identified and carefully managed. To do that, the process must be kept as short as possible, and the key personnel to watch the entire process are needed.

Second, identify and address organizational problems. When data analytics moves onto utilization, collaboration among various divisions is necessary. Data analytics cannot be installed and used easily as in smartphone apps or IT solutions such as office software used in companies. Since the system must be integrated into the activities of the entire company, more people become involved, which impacts the work process. Therefore, data analysts with business-IT competencies must create a program and ensure that it runs on the system easily. Moreover, the data analytics team must operate independently so that there is no interference.

Finally, generate a quick-win. Perform a quick analysis and implement the results. Even a small result can empower data analytics and sustain organizational support. In the early stages, it is also necessary to focus strategically on the part that can give results. Later, provide education and manage changes to ensure results are generated continuously and the model self-grows as data accumulates.

Data Scientist is a Musical Conductor

There is a game in which a team wins when team members relay a sentence, such as a proverb, most accurately while wearing a headphone. As the sentence passes through many people, it ends up changing.

Similarly, errors are generated in the communication process of a big data project. First, business personnel convey their intent from the perspective of utilization. But, IT personnel cannot hear beyond what he can hear despite trying to provide design support. Accordingly, analytics undergo numerous processes and face various challenges and mishaps until results come out. The big data project sometimes ends up producing unintended information, or the company cannot utilize the product of the projects internally due to difference between views of business personnel and IT personnel.

By nature, data analytics does not lend itself to easy verification of errors or precise numeric settlement of items as in accounting management. There are neither correct answers nor easy outcome assessment in data analytics. Consequently, it is difficult to detect when something goes wrong in the process, and more difficult to get intended results.

Especially in large companies, it is difficult to achieve good outcomes of data analytics because they are structured such that the work process is extremely complex, assignments are specialized, and the personnel are focused solely on what they are in charge of. As a result, no one has a comprehensive picture of data analytics. The more complex the process is, the more commonly misunderstandings and errors occur, eventually leading to a failure to produce a good outcome. As mentioned earlier, in data analytics, a small error has a butterfly effect, affecting the outcome.

Communication in the Project

When conducting a big data project, sometimes misinterpretation of analysis results leads to the absence of outcomes due to miscommunication or a difference in background knowledge. The damage is too big to call it a simple communication error. Since utilization of data analytics is an unfamiliar work to employees, they must invest time in learning and must be very familiar with how to use the results.

An online fashion company developed an algorithm to estimate product purchase probability and generate personalized suggested products list using the analysis of customer data. The modeling team instructed the IT team to write a program, a ranking system of purchase probability in which smaller numbers of probability meant higher probability, but the mid-level personnel misinterpreted the probabilities as scores and developed a program that suggested customers products with higher numbers. In the end, purchase rate fell below the previous level (due to the suggestions with lower purchase probabilities), and the company started mistrusting the program, stopped using it, and returned to its earlier way.

In another example, a data analytics team in a global cosmetics company developed a solution that generated the best price by analyzing consumer purchase prices and the range of prices they intend to pay. Then, in their instruction on how to use the solution aimed at those in the field, the data analytics team instructed the use of price suggestions to maximize customer share for young potential VIP customers, and the price suggestions to maximize profitability for older customers. However, those in the field misunderstood and implemented the price policy that maximizes profitability with all customers. As a result, short-term profit somewhat rose, but long-term sales and young customer share significantly fell.

Although being extreme examples, these situations occur more commonly than expected in more complex organizations. In particular, in the organization where work and organization changes fast and turnover is high, there is often a low level of overall understanding, and business and IT blame each other for the lack of results.

Regarding the reason for the lack of results, the personnel in the field argue that the data analytics team developed a poor program, and the system team thinks that those in the field did not use it properly. More-over, the developer attributes it to the problem in the analytics team that designed wrong, and the analytics team attributes it to the mistake in the data team that provided wrong data. All sound plausible, and there is no time to investigate the exact cause. Ultimately, people begin to think, "Let's go back to the previous way so that all share the blame. Then I'll be fine, just doing my own work."

Strategic Intent

The following is an opera conductor's experience. One day, he was trying hard to describe to orchestra members the piece to play in an upcoming performance. He described the bleak situation and the social context the character in the opera was in, and elaborated on the despair their per-formance must express. As he finished the explanation and was about to pick up his baton, a hornist asked grumpily, "I got it, Maestro. So, do you want me to play mezzo forte or forte?"

Reportedly, most members of orchestra lack the knowledge of the details of the opera they play. They neither know nor care how their parts unfold on the stage. Their primary concerns are how much they get paid for practice and how much the lead singer gets.

These days, musicians in the orchestra are viewed as mere parts of the orchestra instead of artists. We can't blame them because they have learnt from their experience that understanding the piece just interferes with playing as they are told.

Similar situations exist in the business world too. The drawback of a system project is that once a system is built, it is turned over to those in the filed in the form of a turn-key (i.e., hand-over in the state in which all systems are operated by a user turning the key at the final stage). Those in the field have little knowledge of the process of building the system and the intention behind the research and creation of the system. Conse-quently, they just take the manual verbatim and do not think hard about the context or background of the contents of the manual.

In a project, I conducted data analytics for an online cosmetics shopping mall company. Based on data analytics, I provided a solution that performs a bundle-product discount strategy on a regular basis by targeting specific customer groups. The strategic intent at the time was as follows. Since the customer group was very sensitive to price, they were willing to make a large purchase at a shopping mall with even a slight advantage in pricing. Accordingly, the strategy to sell in large numbers in a bundle with multiple items to this customer group while offering them at lower price than competitors was chosen.

However, those in the field who were handed over the solution and conducted actual marketing were not informed of this strategy. In an unfortunate coincidence, the concerned cosmetic products were of the brand that could not be bundled. Since they were specified as bundle product discount, the personnel in charge sold the products as discount products individually, thinking that the customer group is sensitive to discount. As a result, they could not sell to the customer group on a large scale, and an unintended customer group reacted like cherry-pickers, worsening profitability.

This was completely different from my intention. Although the focus of the strategy was on bulk sale, the personnel understood it simply as a discount. In this case, they should have improvised the marketing analogous to bundle products such as "buy two for the third one free." However, without knowing the intent of the entire system, it would have been impossible for the personnel to take the approach.

In organizations, employees focus only on their individual responsibilities. It is too much to expect the person who works on his or her assignment passively to understand the overall flow. However, in the current era of big data, the overall outcome is less than good when employees focus only on their own areas. Companies can produce results only when all members of an organization clearly understand the strategic intent. No matter how sophisticated a manual is, it cannot include all possible actions to take when an unanticipated situation occurs.

For a strategy to be implemented successfully, all members of the organization must understand the overall context and operate organically. For this reason, Google operates in small teams of seven to eight members, which makes strategy sharing easy.

Data analysts play the same role as a conductor. They orchestrate various divisions to generate outcomes using results of data analytics. It is for this reason that Google gives full power to most influential data analysts.

Divisions in large companies mostly consider new responsibilities nuisance and are passive about taking them on them. New responsibilities are taken on in a way that do not interfere with their own work. Managing the change in such organizations is also data analysts' responsibility.

Solution 1. Training Data Analysts

As discussed earlier, the fundamental reason that it is difficult for big data to succeed in large companies is because those who analyze and utilize are not the same people. In a complicated task with many stages such as data analytics, the key-man, who has thorough knowledge of the process and fixes the blockages, is essential.

It is rare that business personnel have IT competency or IT personnel have business competency. In general, these two are considered different domains. In fact, business competency and IT competency belong to opposite psychological domains. While business domain concerns aggressive business planning (e.g., marketing, sales, development) primarily based on human psychology, IT competency emphasizes defensive development based on logic, reducing errors, and producing accurate results. They are like the spear and the shield.

Because of this, data analytics faces many challenges in practice. If business personnel have low IT competency, they are pushed around by IT personnel, and if IT personnel have low business competency, the system that is convenient for the IT team but different from the intention of those in the business field is developed.

However, the era of data analytics requires those who are equipped with both competencies and communicate with both departments well. This can be achieved by either providing IT and business personnel with opportunities to experience both aspects to develop the competencies, or bringing external experts in. In the event of training specialists internally, data analytics trainees must be provided with experience working in business rather than just ordinary training, because data analytics based on little experience in business is dead analytics.

In 2014, the introduction to computer science course became the most popular course at Harvard University with 820 students enrolled. It was remarkable that a technology course emerged as the most popular course in the university, but it was more remarkable that the course was known to be difficult to get a good grade in and an elective for most students. The course concerned problem solving using computers. Students learned the way of thinking for logical and efficient problem solving and the method to write program codes using various computer languages.

Why did students become interested in computer programming? Were all Harvard students trying to start a business with software like Mark Zuckerberg? No. They were interested because they knew that they must have coding skills and understand computer science whatever their occupations would be. In the contemporary world of material and information overload, since the roles that take advantage of information like data scientists become increasingly valued, people have reached the conclusion that the domain of software cannot be left solely to IT specialists. To develop data processing skills, it is necessary to have competencies in various areas including business, humanities, IT, and statistics.

Solution 2. Keeping Teams as Small as Possible

Supercell, a Finnish game company well-known for a mobile game *Clash of Clans*, has an estimated company value of about $3.1 billion in 2015. Supercell considers keeping teams as small as possible as the rule of success. It thinks that too much complexity in human and organization processes reduces the probability of success. Launching a game involves a variety of processes including development, performance test, and feature test. In the contemporary world where trends change rapidly, more complex organization and processes have less complexity.

More complexity in a process causes communication problems. Since the size of an organization is proportional to the process of the organization, the size of an organization needs to be reduced, but unfortunately, companies caught up with the idea of large organizations often fail to generate significant results when they establish an organizational system.

Let us be mindful that complication is the sign of aging, one of Parkinson's laws. As an organization becomes more complex, productivity and efficiency of the organization continue to decline. Moreover, big data organizations that must conduct analytics and utilization organically must be small and tight. "A big organism is bound to die," that is, organizations must be small no matter what. This also pertains to organizational issues, to be discussed in the next section.

Corporate Culture as a Barrier to Big Data

In platform-based IT services, speed is more important than sophistication. Competing against high-tech companies with an agile platform while stuck in the shackles of a large corporation is just like having a big handicap at the starting line.

In particular, large offline companies that began as a brick-and-mortar companies have many limitations in providing services in the online environment. Large department stores and supermarkets like JC Penney and Macy's lost the opportunity for long-term growth because they joined the online market too late; offline insurance companies such as State Farm missed getting on the online insurance market bus; and Microsoft did not carry out development of mobile office software due to the issue of controlling the office software market. These are partly influenced by the intention to reduce cannibalization and enter a new market, considering the long-term profit of the companies; however, in most cases, they are caused by the inertia of the corporations.

Competing Interests among Business Divisions

A global sportswear company conducted data analytics to establish marketing plans. The results of the data analytics showed that the needs for famous high-end products were growing rapidly in developing countries, where the supply could not catch up with the demand. Therefore, the priority was to choose a major distributor in the developing countries and distribute the products quickly. Accordingly, the marketing team requested for product procurement and research on distributors.

But this request was rejected. The reason was primarily because of the low status of IT and marketing teams in the company. Company-wide support is necessary for implementing strategies, but company politics often makes it impossible to persuade the officers of the companies. This occurs because of the inertia of the organization, that is, motivation to focus only on one's own division such as sales and logistics, or avoiding taking a risk, thinking it as others' business. Even when one or more

officers support the plans, if there are many who have conflicting interests due to divisional responsibilities, the implementation can stumble
because of others' jealousy or control. Organizational culture may cause
conflicts or excessive constraints. In the end, even great strategies that can
generate positive outcomes are frequently left unimplemented and things
are done using conventional approaches.

Data analytics does not always generate results just in the form of
IT solutions such as program modifications, system building, and automation. It sometimes requires support from all areas such as sales, production, logistics, and R&D in addition to a full span of marketing. In
such cases, it takes tremendous courage and drive to convince numerous
people who have different interests to utilize the results of data analytics.
Therefore, despite many results of data analytics and marketing plans that
are generated, large corporations often do not execute them.

The Law of Inertia

A global IT company that requested me to provide consultation poured in
tens of millions of dollars in building a data analytics marketing system,
but the company was found to have conducted no marketing event for a
year since the system was built. It advertised big data by dressing it up as a
tremendous system, but the efforts fizzled out in the end. Most marketing
divisions of large corporations put a lot of effort in research, analysis, and
planning, but the results are wasted, not having been executed.

Marketing teams are reluctant to execute. The same is true of data analytics teams too. In a company, the worst case scenario for an employee is
to be fired. How to avoid the worst case scenario? Do not execute results.
All divisions in most companies including sales, marketing, and production have a tendency to do things in the way they have been done. That
is, they make as few new attempts as possible. This is why they create a
system by making a huge preparation and investment, but which does not
get used in practice. The risk of failure (here, being fired) is bigger than
the benefit of doing well by executing it. In other words, employees gain
more by pleasing superiors than generating profits for the company.

Companies never change their existing ways unless they are about
to fail. But, when the situation is dire enough, it is already too late. As

existing market declines, companies stick to the market, decline together, and meet the same fate as the market. This is the common thread that runs through the process of the downfall of large corporations such as RadioShack, Nokia, and JC Penney that once dominated the world.

This is the reason why the successful cases of big data analytics are rare—companies have not implemented the results of analytics. Neither the IT team nor the marketing team wants to execute the unverified results because of the fear of generating poor outcome. How can the results be verified if no one implements them? This is the very reason why companies just publicize that they "found a growth potential" or they are "innovative companies that use state-of-art technology" while disclosing the results of small tests or curious statistics.

Solution 1. Change in the Management Team

To combine management with the somewhat unfamiliar data analytics, the management team must have high level of understanding of big data and provide a strong support to big data analytics.

An IT team of a large fashion retail company conducted data analytics for marketing. The results of data analytics showed that there are significant needs for multi-brand online stores and large SPAs targeting working women. The analytics system generated in real time product designs and brands that are expected to be popular and identified the brands for the multi-brand stores. It was time for upgrading online shopping malls and preparing to launch an offline SPA.

However, this was not carried out after all. The biggest reason was the indifference of the management. The top management consisted primarily of those who had achieved results through brand merchandizing or sales, and they doubted the effects of multi-brand stores and SPAs due to a bias toward traditional fashion retail, and accordingly, a lack of understanding of the new approaches in business. In the end, the company missed the opportunity to take the control of the new market and the growth slowed down.

Moreover, as the company was publically traded and the ownership and the management became separated, the management became increasingly too wrapped up with short-term financial performance. The management did not take the business approach they did not know well and did not want to handover the management control. To their eyes, the IT team was just a single support team and online was a small distribution network.

In most companies, people often define the IT team as playing a mere supporting role for key divisions as described above. If the management does not understand data analytics and is passive about supporting it, data analytics can never produce positive outcomes. Since data analytics is significantly influenced by the capacity of the management, convincing the management is essential. The success of most companies hinges upon the transformation of the management.

Solution 2. Independent Division with a Clear Role and Authority

Large organizations have the strength of being stable, but they also have the weakness of being conservative. Conservative organizational culture limits creativity. How can we solve this conservative organization problem? The solution is to create an independent team backed by the initiative of the management.

"Build a Bunker that Can Stand Against External Attacks."

Tesco, which made a success story of the loyalty club card using consumer analysis, also initially faced much opposition. Most officers of the company at the time viewed the strange membership program and customer data analysis as just a waste of resources. However, considering data analytics as the company's core competency, Tesco's CEO decided to incubate it by investing company resources.

Accordingly, the CEO organized a project team called "The Bunker" using his strong initiative, isolated from other divisions. Then, he instructed the team to conduct an independent analysis of customers and develop services without external influences. He believed that conducting data analytics project despite opposition from certain retailers and sales and marketing personnel was necessary for the company's long-term future. Eventually, conducting a marketing based on a unique analytic model, Tesco was able to take control of the retail market in the UK, making up for a short-term decline in performance.

An organization is an organism. It must change according to the constantly changing business environment. A rigid organization is a dead organization. Therefore, a strategic organizer needs to keep the organization organically orderly through constant communication.

As much as focus of organizations was on sales and production in the past, what is needed now to adapt to the current data-based business is a change in the organization based on marketing and data platform. This can be achieved by clarifying the authority and responsibilities of data analytics-based strategic teams and establishing a team structure that can accentuate strengths of individuals.

Contemporary global IT service companies have a strong tendency to incubate small, independent teams within the companies. For the same reason, in the Silicon Valley, technology-based independent, small venture companies grow better than large companies with a long history. This is because only independent organizations can be free from external pressure and focus on goals.

Generally, IT divisions in companies take on a variety of tasks. As they work on various tasks, data analytics are often put on a back burner because it does not affect business and business personnel immediately like system failures does. Thus, data analytics is gradually pushed back from the center of interest, and IT divisions often end up occasionally performing shallow analysis.

To make all processes of data analytics operate actively, an independent data analytics team with a clearly defined goal must be organized and given necessary authority. At the same time, steady consensus building activities with other divisions are necessary to develop data analytics as the core competency of the company.

Importance of Quick-Win Can Never Be Overstated

In 2014, Zulily.com, a US online shopping mall, reported $1.2 billion net sales, with an estimated net value twice that of Groupon. Zulily presents machine learning, data processing, and analytics technology as the core competencies of the company. It provides personalized services using data analytics ranging from millions of website design, to advertisement e-mails, to mobile apps, and to product composition. Zulily is considered an exemplar of data analytics in various areas ranging from big data analytics to outcomes. Did Zulily grow based on huge capital from the beginning?

Bowling alley strategy

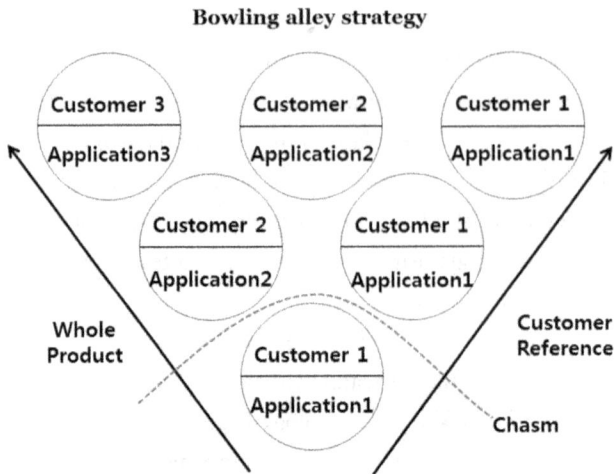

Founded in 2010, Zulily began as a small social commerce company that primarily sold baby care products. They initially had difficulty expanding business due to the lack of business partners and data. Accordingly, Zulily decided to target young mothers with distinctive styles and strong influence, and focused on providing the products and brands they wanted.

Later, as customers grew through word-of-mouth and data accumulated, they began personalized marketing based on data analytics. Gradually, name brands joined Zulily one by one, and sales volume and product groups continually grew. A virtuous cycle of stronger analytic capability with growing data began. Since its foundation in 2010, Zulily accomplished over 100 percent sales growth every year, and the engine behind it was none other than "quick-win."

Among marketing theories, there is a theory called the bowling alley strategy—striking the bowling pin at the front makes the pins behind fall one by one. In other words, when there is a quick-win, the profit is reinvested to expand the market. This strategy allows venture companies with weak capital to expand business without a risk if they can achieve quick-win. In the current B2C industries, heavy initial investment can never be a good strategy.

One of Google's mottos is "Think big, but start small." Drawing a big picture is very important. But in real business, there are too many risks in the execution process. Therefore, acting fast leads to success in the long-term.

Doubts on Big Data

A retail company had requested me to provide consultation on big data analytics. I explained to the management previous results of data analytics to convince them of the effectiveness of data analytics prior to the launch of the project; but most of the management was skeptical about the results of big data analytics. They mostly argued: "The unique aspects of our company are different. Even though you had results in other cases, this one might be difficult."; "This is different from what I have been doing. The success depends absolutely on sales, and the only way to achieve results is to keep moving to meet customers." or, "Do you have any experience with this industry? I've been in this industry for decades, and data marketing has never succeeded."

Facing these responses, I moved up the schedule for the pilot project. Since they were not persuaded, no matter how hard I tried to convince them, it was best to show them results. As I announced the results after finishing marketing planning, and execution and analysis, the management that witnessed the results increased two fold finally acknowledged the effect of data analytics. With the support of the management, the project proceeded without interference, and the module based on big data was utilized in a variety of areas including marketing, merchandising, and sales.

Elite data analytics team does not guarantee success. How can it address the problem of the management that often has a doubt on effectiveness of data analytics? It is in some ways natural that the management does not understand the logic of data analytics and is not convinced it will work. They lack the background knowledge and experience of management, statistics, and information technology. This cannot be resolved with just a few rounds of explanations.

First of all, the project must demonstrate the results fast, even if on a small scale. Once witnessing the result, the management changes their attitude, tries to understand more proactively, and provides full support. Then, the virtuous cycle begins—supporting data analytics, and raising the status of the team.

Neofect, a data-based medical venture company, initially experienced a great difficulty in garnering investment from venture capital. Their approach of increasing the effect of learning by detecting movements of stroke patients and providing comprehensive treatment program using data analytics was not convincing to experts in the medical industry and investors. Despite extensive efforts with logical explanations, investors showed no interest.

Upon receiving the request for consultation from Neofect, I proposed an approach to produce results with two stages. The first stage was to demonstrate clinical effects with experimental results on patients, and the second stage was to show the financial results of their product after purchases by well-known hospitals, institutions, and rehabilitation centers. The former was to show the quick-win to consumers, while the latter was to show the quick-win to investors.

Neofect conducted clinical experiments as a priority and demonstrated the effects by publishing the results in credible journals. Consumers who learned the news tested the product of Neofect and were satisfied with its effectiveness. Then, Neofect sold the product to well-known hospitals including the National Rehabilitation Center and Samsung Medical Center generating revenue. Seeing the potential of the company, investors ran to the company with strong interest in investment, and Neofect went on the growth trajectory as they garnered investments in favorable terms and recruited highly qualified personnel.

It is difficult for small startups to get in a virtuously cycle. Since they often get in the vicious cycle of lack of capital, status, and talents, they are likely to get off the track toward making money, and as a result, the situation of the company worsens. What venture capital companies consider most important when they consider investing is whether sales are made. In other words, however small it is, if the key product is sold, the company is recognized as the company with a potential. Conversely, it means that it is just as much difficult to achieve quick-win, and quick-wins are a must in big data analytics.

Without a quick-win, data analytics must go through a long arduous process. Therefore, do not try to hit a jackpot but focus on getting quick-win. Then, the next stage will resolve itself. To produce a quick-win, it is necessary to have many trials and errors, even small ones, which I will discuss next.

Must Fail to Succeed

Angry Birds, a famous smartphone game, did not show any sign of hitting a jackpot in the early stages of its development. It was a crude version with no marketability at the beginning, but the Angry Birds that we know now was born as a result of incremental improvements during development.

The developer of Angry Birds, Rovio, followed these three tenets: "If a failure is unavoidable, let's fail early"; "There should be no significant risk associated with failure"; and "Failure must contribute to success." The way Rovio became successful was to float a game on a server, get feedback from the public, make a quick change, and float a modified game.

Let us apply this process to data analytics. Although it is important to prepare thoroughly, realistically speaking, it is impossible to eliminate all risks in advance. If data analytics is complete to an extent, the results must be quickly put into practice to eliminate uncertainty; no practice, no success. If a goal is to produce a quick-win, results must be quickly executed.

The Basics of the Strategy is "Quantity over Quality, and Speed over Accuracy."

Prior to the execution of the results of data analytics, they go through many ups and downs. Problem-solving principles and strategies established based on insights gained from data analysis may generate numerous execution plans, and executions and outcomes are two different things. It is fine to explore the possibility of success by performing various additional analyses before execution; however, in practice, it is often the case that the outcome can be known only through the execution in the field. Therefore, unless the risk for execution is high, it is better to execute earlier rather than later. The most common reason for the failure of big data is not because analysis is not sharp, but because of the inability to stand the process in the execution stage. Let us not fear the failure of execution. We only need a handful of plans that produce the outcome anyway.

Ticketmonster, a leading social commerce company in Korea, utilizes the AB test actively in registering and placing products and deciding on promotions and prices. What is the advantage of the AB test? In general, when a marketing strategy is implemented, it is impossible to clearly establish the experimental and the control groups, and it is also difficult

Problem-solving	Strategizing	Execution plan	Execution	Outcome

Plan 1 - - - - - - -> X

Plan 2 - - - ->X

Case, Idea

Hypothesis   **Solution (Strategic Intent)**   Plan 3 - - - - - - - - - - -> O

Plan 4   X

Data Verification   Plan 5 - - - - - - - - -↘ O

Plan 6 - - - ->X

....

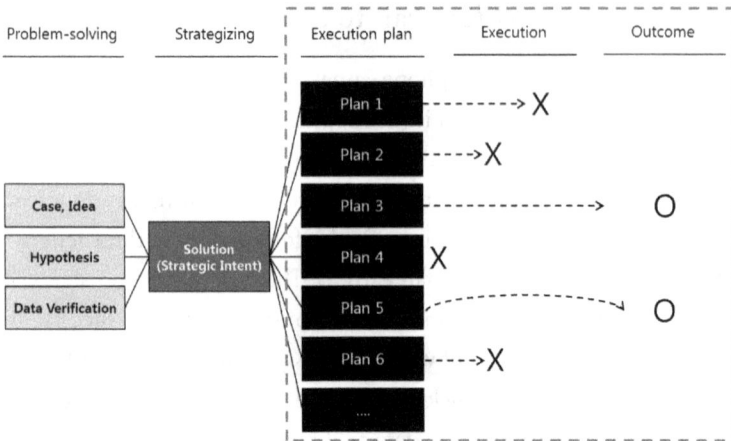

to measure the financial outcome of the marketing plan. However, the AB test can produce results quickly and it allows clear comparison of the results. Showing the results quickly through the AB test can also help fast decision making.

Case study
The Danger of Too Idealistic Goals

"Let's work toward world peace."

Who would oppose this call? No one; everyone would agree. The problem is to do with how to go about it. Instead of putting forward an empty slogan, one must work hard to think of how to go about it and put it into practice.

The same goes for data analytics. Many technology enthusiasts often set up a highly idealistic goal (e.g., "Let's optimize personalized marketing with machine learning technology!"), face difficulties right from the beginning, and get frustrated. Data analytics is useless unless it actually works and generates value. Nevertheless, many IT and statistics experts do research from an idealistic and conceptual standpoint, and neglect to work on how to apply it to real life.

A fashion retail company created a project of sending out coupons continuously and analyzing them, to determine the optimal promotion amount to make it personalized for individual customers. The plan was to find the optimal coupon amount that each customer responds to and maximize profitability by giving out $3 coupons and raising the amount if the customer does not respond, and lowering the amount if the customer responds. At first glance, this looked plausible, so no one objected and the project was launched with great anticipation of success.

However, the project ultimately failed. Optimizing the amount was meaningless because the personalized optimal coupon amount kept changing, and there were too many customers whose results were impossible to interpret—for instance, not purchasing when a $5 coupon was provided, while purchasing when a $3 coupon was provided. These occurred probably because of other factors and insufficient data.

From a customer's point of view, tens of factors influence product purchase, including competition, timing, individual circumstances, and trends. It is impossible to remove all these variables and set up "coupon amount" as an independent variable. In the context of a lack of clearly defined experimental and control groups, it was too much of a leap of faith to conclude that the presence or absence of purchase was due to the coupon amount.

Moreover, trying to understand coupon issuance and result data at the individual level was like judging a person by his or her silhouette. The purchase history of an individual is very scant. Determining an individual's profile based on this data has too much scope for error. But we have much more data than this. It becomes much more accurate if we group customers into meaningful types and understand the big data through these types. The best part of big data analysis is that individual data can be assembled to indicate a greater meaning. Ignoring this aspect and analyzing the individual unit cannot but generate errors and be ineffective.

Making a quick-win lies in translating an ideal into a realistic goal. One must be cautious against being too idealistic, ending up with failure, and losing the determination to continue.

To summarize, big data analytics are rarely executed because of the "inertia of organization" as discussed earlier, which can be solved by a quick-win to ensure a secure position for big data. Therefore, it is necessary to quickly conduct a small-scale, feasible analysis and execution that would not pose a significant risk in the event of failure, to get a fast result.

In an offline environment, in the past, even one execution could be a significant burden; however, in the current online environment, execution does not pose as serious a risk. An agile driving force in development and execution is the key to success.

Further Study: Amazon's Cloud Service and Walmart's Express Store

Amazon's mission statement states, "Our vision is to be earth's most customer centric company; to build a place where people can come to find and discover anything they might want to buy online." Amazon is a customer-centered retail company. However, unlike other retail companies, Amazon also provides B2B cloud service (Amazon Web Services). Amazon's cloud services were making profits enough to account for about one-third of the net sales profit of Amazon in 2015. In the context of the traditional management strategic perspective that expansion to other industries must be avoided (because the core competency is distributed), what was Amazon's intention?

Although being in a retail industry, Amazon is originally a company based on platform technology. It was most important to expertly build and operate the environment in which consumers and vendors meet. Later, as they raised the service quality through selecting and managing vendors, identifying consumers' needs and expanding supply, they got on the virtuous cycle and were able to take control of the market.

In this process, Amazon was able to secure large database management technology and sophisticated consumer marketing algorithms. These two are Amazon's core competencies. Based on the database management technology, Amazon launched the cloud services as the new business, and this is making large profits in the growing market.

Although in the same retail industry, Walmart's move was the opposite. Walmart expanded its Express Store service on a large scale. It entered the neighborhood market, the consumer contact point, from a macroeconomic perspective. This shows an intention to expand its area drastically and showcase the economies of scale and consumer-friendly services rather than remaining as only a large retailer. On the other hand, it has not showed clear signs of customer service using platform-based IT technology yet. Why?

The core competency of Walmart is its large network and product sourcing capability. Having started with meeting the low-price purchase needs using mass production through a close relationship with vendors, Walmart accumulated cost-saving strategies and knowhow. Based on these, it identified customer needs and expanded throughout the US. Then, in order to make it bigger, it expanded to being the neighborhood market. Although Walmart is a retail company, its core competency is closer to cost efficiency based on economies of scale. Therefore, it was a natural progression that Walmart took the approach in a traditional manufacturing-retail-logistics aspect rather than take on platform technology and analytics algorithms that they were weak in.

Human cannot walk in two directions simultaneously. The same goes for companies. If they try to solve many things with a single core competency (brain), many constraints and inefficiency occur. Companies make progresses around the core competencies they have developed since their foundation, and once they get on the growth trajectory, they require a shift in core competency, and this process produce challenges.

A significant part of the shift in companies' core competencies these days is probably a shift toward data analytics-based platforms and algorithms. In the current world of continuing advances in automation and machine learning technologies, just ad hoc strategies or short-term sales are not enough for companies to survive. If the corporate system does not become accustomed to algorithms, companies will eventually fall behind. Therefore, it is time to prepare to compete in the global market by avoiding a zero-sum game focusing on increasing the size, and converting data utilization competency and knowledge knowhow into assets.

What is the reason for large companies such as GE and Ford to have difficulties in online and service industries? Although many contributing factors exist, organizational culture has a significant impact. The core competencies of companies develop into the organizational culture. The culture of technology-based venture companies that succeed even if one out of 1,000 strategies succeeds, is very different from the culture of manufacturing companies that suffer great damages if even one out of 1,000 products is defective. No matter how hard a manufacturing company tries to create a horizontal structure and an environment to respect the uniqueness of individual business operations in order to evolve into a service company, problems occur due to factors such as differing interests among divisions and different business mindsets at the higher level. Just as it is difficult to change core competencies, deep-rooted organizational culture does not change easily. It does not change just because a few officers of the company call for it. Companies need to take a quantum leap to shift their mindsets quickly through innovation rather than follow global IT companies such as Google and Facebook with only a vague idea of what to do.

The current global business environment is changing into the environment of identifying individual needs and working in small teams with diversity and freedom, adapting to the material and information overload in the contemporary world. Data analytics is essentially an activity to identify human needs and meet them, and achieving a change in the business environment from a macroscopic perspective is also necessary for the success of big data.

EPILOGUE

"I don't trust big data."

Although many companies say they recognize the importance of big data, leaders of the companies often share this secret in person: "Big data is overrated and does not help deliver value to customers. It looks like something, but has no substance." This is an argument against the utility of big data from an expert who has produced results in the field.

There are many people who do not trust the effectiveness of big data. In particular, after experiencing that data analytics produced no results in the field, they become completely dismissive about utilizing data analytics. Field experts think of big data enthusiasts as "techno-buffs who never produced the results" or as "ardent rooky reformists."

According to my experience, whether they have actually utilized data analytics or not, people have many preconceptions about data analytics. Different industries and companies have different types, sizes, and depths of data, analytic capability, timing in utilization, and approaches. Big data is like a knife. When a sharp knife is held by a mother's hand, it becomes a cooking tool to make a nice meal, but when it is used by a robber, it becomes a dangerous tool for a crime. In the same way, big data also leads to completely opposite outcomes depending on the person who uses it and the purpose of its use. Therefore, we cannot decide if data analytics is a success or a failure by thinking about it based on just a single aspect.

In the past, due to the low level of information gathered and a lack of skills in utilizing data analytics, it was difficult to produce results in the field using data analytics. However, the present time is literally an "era of big data." Various recognition technologies of human activities are making advances, and the complexity of recorded data has grown significantly. As specifications of hardware have become increasingly sophisticated, storage capacity and processing performance have also been enhanced significantly. In the future, nearly all human activities are expected to be recorded and stored as data using ubiquitous technology.

How about software analytic technology? The Hadoop-based distributed processing platform has opened the door to big data analytics by overcoming the limitations of structured data analytics based on conventional mainframe servers.

Now only the utilization of data and tools is left for humans to do. Utilizing data using our brains is the only task left for humans to do, since this cannot be done by robots or algorithms.

Many are concerned that big data looks dazzling, but has no substance. It is confusing whether big data refers to social data, or the data accumulated by companies, or mobile data, and whether it refers to all weblogs or only unstructured data, because there is no consensus on the issue. It is also unclear whether big data business refers to solution development, application development, system building, or strategy building.

However, it does not have to be complicated. Big data just literally means a large amount of data, and producing results using this data is the challenge we face. Big data is just a paradigm of modern civilization, and we just need to make human lives better using big data.

Winning the big data war depends no longer on the ability to make sophisticated hardware, but hinges upon software capabilities. The key competitive edge and what generates growth is the creation of value by analyzing big data.

I also once underestimated the value of data analytics while consulting on various corporate strategies. The reason behind it was that it was so difficult to produce decent outcomes using data analytics. Most corporate culture is actually operated by the CEO, a decision maker, and key personnel in industrial technology. No companies consider IT services as their core competency. IT divisions play a supporting role of making the work process more efficient and automated, and have little influence on business. Therefore, IT divisions also provide only the required services passively and defensively, rather than developing innovative capabilities. Since organizational culture itself is not ready to meet the needs for retaining soft power, the gap between business and IT naturally emerges, while skepticism about the utility of data analytics prevails, and only the outdated management style persists.

It is extremely difficult for an oversized corporate structure to change culture and develop soft power. No one has the courage to let go of power and the source of money. Organizational culture does not change easily by a few people calling for it. In many companies, due to the large corporation style management environment, most of the talents with soft skills either are unable to exercise their creativity, or do no more than developing simple mobile apps or games.

Since the dawn of the 2010s, the way businesses operate has changed completely. The coercive style of management that originated from the rigid organizations in the manufacturing industry revealed its limitations, and it became clear that soft power is the only way to survive in the current global market. In the global competition, more and more companies experience the limitations of oversized inefficient organization and look for changes and innovation.

I have conducted big data analytics projects based on strategies by selecting companies that can produce results. Using my guidance on establishing and executing big data analytics, companies were able to develop competitiveness and produce results in the end after many trials and errors. This book is the essence of such experiences, and I hope that the personnel in big data analytics read this book and find it helpful.

To reiterate, big data is the key growth engine in the future that companies' survival depends on. I have paid special attention to writing a practical book that can be used in the big data war zone right away, instead of writing a theoretical book on big data methodology. Every word in this book reflects my determination to help your big data analytics succeed. It is my sincere desire that everyone creates value and happiness by digging the gold mine called data.

Patrick
2016

About the Author

Written by Patrick H. Park, the author of *Brain Work* (2014), this book mainly focuses on why data analytics fail in business. It provides an objective analysis and explains the root causes of the phenomenon, instead of making an abstract criticism of the utility of data analytics. The author then explains in detail how companies can survive and win the global big data competition, based on actual case studies of companies.

Having established the execution and performance-oriented big data methodology based on over 10 years of experience in the field as an authority in big data strategy, the author identifies the core principles of data analytics using case analyses of failures and successes of actual companies. Moreover, he endeavors to share with readers the principles of how innovative global companies became successful through the utilization of big data. This book is a quintessential **guide to** big data analytics, in which the author's know-how learnt from direct and indirect experiences is condensed.

How do we survive this big data war, in which Facebook in social network services (SNS), Amazon in e-commerce, and Google in web-search, expand their platforms to other areas based on their respective distinct markets? The answer can be found in this book.

Patrick H. Park

Park graduated from Korea University and received his MBA from Darden School of Business at the University of Virginia. He worked as a data analytics expert in a venture capital firm in New York City, and as a top authority in big data strategy in a global management consulting company. He established a performance based big data methodology based on over 10 years of experience in the field. His methodology, which executes the entire process starting from big data strategy building to system design, development, and utilization, has successfully been used in major companies and research institutes.

He has served as a columnist in business management for a major economic newspaper in Korea, and is conducting research on corporate big data technology, as an industry-academic cooperation professor at Catholic University. More recently, he presented "Performance-oriented Data analytics" in CRM Fair. He currently serves as a management consultant and outside director for leading companies, and is the CEO of Value Management Group, a performance-oriented strategy consulting network. His previous publications include *Brain Work* (2014).

Index

OTHER TITLE IN OUR BIG DATA AND BUSINESS ANALYTICS COLLECTION

Mark Ferguson, University of South Carolina, *Editor*

- *Business Intelligence and Data Mining* by Anil Maheshwari
- *Data Mining Models* by David Olson

FORTHCOMING TITLES FOR THIS COLLECTION

- *Predictive Analytics: An Introduction to Big Data, Data Mining, and Text Mining* by Barry Keating
- *Business Location Analytics: The Research and Marketing Strategic Advantage* by David Z. Beitz
- *Business Analytics: A Data-Driven Decision Making Approach for Business* by Amar Sahay

Announcing the Business Expert Press Digital Library

Concise e-books business students need for classroom and research

This book can also be purchased in an e-book collection by your library as

- *a one-time purchase,*
- *that is owned forever,*
- *allows for simultaneous readers,*
- *has no restrictions on printing, and*
- *can be downloaded as PDFs from within the library community.*

Our digital library collections are a great solution to beat the rising cost of textbooks. E-books can be loaded into their course management systems or onto students' e-book readers. The **Business Expert Press** digital libraries are very affordable, with no obligation to buy in future years. For more information, please visit **www.businessexpertpress.com/librarians**. To set up a trial in the United States, please email **sales@businessexpertpress.com**.

www.ingramcontent.com/pod-product-compliance
Lightning Source LLC
Chambersburg PA
CBHW072308210326
41519CB00057B/3095